THE EVER-LOVING
TRUTH

THE EVER-LOVING
TRUTH

CAN FAITH THRIVE IN A POST-CHRISTIAN CULTURE?

VODDIE BAUCHAM, JR.

B&H
PUBLISHING GROUP

NASHVILLE, TENNESSEE

Copyright © 2004
by Voddie Baucham
All rights reserved
Printed in the United States of America

ISBN: 978-0-8054-2788-2

Published by B&H Publishing Group,
Nashville, Tennessee

Dewey Decimal Classification: 270.83
Subject Heading: DISCIPLESHIP \
CHRISTIANS—PERSECUTIONS \
CHRISTIANITY AND CURRENT ISSUES

Unless otherwise indicated, Scripture quotations are from the New
American Standard Bible, © the Lockman Foundation,
1960, 1962, 1963, 1968, 1971, 1972, 1973, 1975, 1977; used
by permission. Other versions are identified as follows:
NIV, the Holy Bible, New International Version, copyright © 1973,
1978, 1984 by International Bible Society. NKJV, New King
James Version, copyright © 1979, 1980, 1982, Thomas Nelson,
Inc., Publishers. Italic in Scripture text has been by the
author for emphasis.

16 17 18 19 20   18 17 16 15 14

To the love of my life, Bridget

My Proverbs 31 woman,
the mother, and teacher of my children,
and my partner in preparing them
to impact the culture for the cause of Christ

CONTENTS

PREFACE

Truth is under attack in our culture. The person who believes in ideas, concepts, values, or facts that are true for all people in all places for all times is rare, indeed. One is much more likely to hear the new cliché, "That may be true for you, but it is not necessarily true for me." Gone are the days when right and wrong were black and white. Today's morality is painted in shades of gray. Same-sex unions are a reality in Vermont; the concept of creation is not allowed to share space in the classroom with the tenuous, unsupported theory of evolution; Ten Commandments displays are under attack in the public square; the pledge of allegiance has been brought into question in California; and the Christmas holiday has become a "winter break." Where will it all end? Or better yet, where did it begin?

This book is the result of what seems like a lifelong search to answer these and other questions about the way our culture has taught us to think (or not to think). Much of what has become readily accepted in the marketplace of ideas is not only unbiblical but in many instances utterly illogical. However, this is not new. Much of what we are experiencing in post-Christian America is eerily similar to what the early church experienced in pre-Christian Rome.

Peter and John were marginalized for their reliance upon unorthodox argumentation; modern Christians are accused of "checking their minds at the church door" or "committing intellectual suicide" for believing the Bible. Peter and John were forbidden to speak or teach in the name of Jesus; modern American Christians face the same injunction. The similarities are striking.

Unfortunately, however, the similarities tend to cease when it comes to the apostles' response. They challenged their culture; we tend to conform to ours. They embraced the sovereignty of God in the midst of their persecution; we question the sovereignty of God in ours. They considered it a privilege to suffer for the cause of Christ; we have been conditioned to view it as punishment. Our response to the post-Christian culture in which we live leaves quite a bit to be desired.

I had a conversation with a pastor friend not long ago. He asked me about the subject of the book he had heard I was working on. When I told him, he replied, "I've got one for you." He began to tell me about an interesting Sunday night Bible study he had led a few weeks earlier. He was teaching through 1 Corinthians, and he had come to chapter 5. The young people, as was their practice, were sitting in a group down front. He was especially sensitive to their whereabouts, as he knew that the discussion of the man in the text who had been involved in an illicit affair with his stepmother would intrigue them.

Much to the pastor's surprise, it was not the idea of the illicit affair that intrigued the crowd but the idea that Paul would have the audacity to suggest to the church at Corinth that they should have removed him from their midst. That was the part of the text that the crowd found most disturbing. Many of those present—both young and old—could not believe that Paul said, "I have already passed judgment on the one who did this." The pastor, upon sensing the discomfort in the room, asked for input from the group. He was not surprised when one of the young people said, "I thought we weren't supposed to judge." He was, however, surprised when one of the older members—a leader in the church—stated, "I don't care what the Bible says; we are not supposed to judge other people!"

The pastor was aghast. He pressed the point. He used Scripture, logic, everything he could think of to make his point. He even went to the oft-misquoted and misunderstood passage in Matthew 7 and addressed the misconception. Nothing got through. No one was willing to say that what the man in the text had done was right. Nevertheless, no one was willing to agree with the actions of Paul.

I had a similar encounter after a message I preached from the fourteenth chapter of John. Immediately following the service, a woman came barreling toward me. She had no problem with the part of the text which taught that Jesus was preparing a place in his Father's house for those who follow him. She did, however, have, in her words, "a serious problem with the idea that Jesus is the only way." She spoke in a sympathetic yet condescending tone, as though she were making me aware of what must have been a monumental oversight on my part. However, her sympathy and condescension quickly turned to outrage and disbelief when I assured her that I meant to say exactly what I said, and exactly the way I said it. She said she couldn't understand how I, of all people, "could be so narrow-minded."

The key to understanding these and other such encounters is to understand the philosophical assumptions that serve as the backdrop to much of people's thinking. Many in our culture have been conditioned to sift all religious discussions through the colander of religious relativism, tolerance, and philosophical pluralism. These are the ideas that lead to statements such as, "We all worship the same God," "All religions are equal," and that oft-voiced question, "Who are we to judge others?" The beliefs behind these words have led us to consider those who have strong religious convictions as having "checked their minds at the door."

I assert that nothing could be further from the truth. There is a God, and that God has revealed himself. Therefore, if we have access to that revelation, we have access to truth—the kind that is true for all people, in all places, at all times—truth that is absolute. This does not give those of us who know this God a license to be arrogant, rude, or obnoxious. On the contrary, it gives us an obligation to speak the truth in love.

Pre-Christian Attitudes in a Post-Christian Culture

Several years ago I had the privilege of preaching to a group of college students from across the United States. The person who had extended the invitation simply requested that I address these students "where they live." He knew that I was enamored with the art and science of apologetics, so he suggested that I pick an issue and have at it.

As I anticipated the event, I began to go over past experiences and conversations with college students in my mind. Several themes emerged. One recurring theme was the conversation with the antagonistic college professor. Many students have asked me the same question over the years: "What do I say to a professor who insists on demeaning my faith in class?" Another theme was the attack by anti-Christian campus groups. Christian groups are often prime targets for campus organizations bent on secular-humanistic or even pagan worldviews. Yet another theme in these conversations over the years has centered on what constitutes a legal expression of religious faith. Students wanted to know if they could wear clothing with Christian themes, if they could decorate the doors of their dorm rooms for Christmas, or if they could hold Christian services on campus. In other words, Where is the mysterious line of separation between church and state?

As I began to prepare, I knew I could not tackle all of the issues. I also knew that I didn't want to turn this into a lecture. So I began to search for a passage of Scripture that would address the core of the problem. As I searched I had one of those "ah-hah" moments. I began reading in Acts chapter 4, and all of the pieces came together. There it was in black and white. Peter and John were not just first-century believers being harassed for their faith by an antagonistic culture; they were prototypes. It was as though their experience foreshadowed the experiences of the college students to whom I spoke. Furthermore, the assumptions that precipitated the antagonism they encountered were very similar to those present in our current cultural milieu.

Since then I have become more keenly aware of not just what our culture thinks about Christians and Christianity, but why they think it. From Ten Commandment displays to the pledge of allegiance, we see the inevitable results of a philosophical shift that has gradually altered the religious landscape of our society. Fortunately, this is nothing new. The early church overcame pre-Christian attitudes and left us a blueprint with which we can evaluate, infiltrate, and invade our culture with *The Ever-Loving Truth.*

1
WHO ARE THESE UNTRAINED MEN?

When my wife and I first married as college students, we were "po"—so poor that we couldn't afford the second *o* and the *r* in the word, as the old joke goes.

We had nothing. Nothing, that is, except a couple of pieces of hand-me-down furniture. One was a couch that my mother had given us. She had earlier reupholstered it in a tan fabric, and it had three large cushions that were adorned with a series of orange squares set inside larger brown squares. It was hideous! Nevertheless, we were proud to have it. We kept that couch for several years.

Eventually, we both graduated from college and went from "po" to poor, and gradually we progressed to being merely broke. As we moved up the socioeconomic ladder, we began to acquire new furniture—first a coffee table, then a couple of bar stools, a dining room table, and a large floor lamp. Things were really looking up! However, the couch remained. I don't know if it was the prohibitive cost of buying a new couch or the fact that my mother had recovered it herself before she gave it to us, but the couch lingered on.

Then it happened. The moment of truth arrived. We looked around and realized that there was a new theme in our home décor. The apartment had taken on a "poor-man's modern" look. Everything was beginning to come together—everything, that is, except the couch. The couch stood out like a beggar at a black-tie dinner. Something had to be done! The couch had to go.

At first we didn't have the heart to throw it out. Nor could we give it away. It had been a gift and a reminder of humble beginnings. So we decided to put it in an extra room. After a while, though, the couch was no longer good enough for that room, either. The time had come. It had to go. We did what was once unthinkable: we got up one morning and waited for the trash collector. When he arrived, I took the long walk out to the curb, where I said my final good-byes. He threw it into the truck, and it was gone.

You may be thinking about the title of this book and asking yourself, "What does this little story have to do with living in a post-Christian world?" Our old couch is also a poignant illustration of the thesis of this book. You see, in many ways, Christianity has become to our culture what that couch became to my family.

There was a time when American culture looked favorably upon Christianity. In fact, Chief Justice John Jay once referred to America as a Christian nation. There is no doubt that the founders of this great nation built it upon biblical principles. But things have changed.

We now live in what has commonly been referred to as "post-Christian" America. In fact, there are many who wish to purge America of any Christian influence. It sometimes seems as though someone in power woke up one day and said, "Christianity was useful once, even important and comfortable for a while, but it doesn't fit our needs anymore. It's fine to practice your faith at church, but keep it out of the marketplace of ideas." Some go further than wanting Christianity to be less visible; they are openly antagonistic. Christians in America are finding themselves in an increasingly hostile environment.

This state of affairs is nothing new for the church. Throughout history Christians have been the targets of ridicule and persecution. While there are lessons to be learned from the suffering and endurance of our contemporaries, it is always best to begin with believers who have gone before us—those who are a part of the historical record and whose stories have been provided, protected, and preserved in the Bible.

One such story is that of Peter and John before the Sanhedrin (Acts 4:1–31). In their interrogation we can observe the onset of Christian persecution. In fact, the questioning of the two apostles takes a path similar to that of the persecution of Christians who have come after them. The Acts account also gives us insight into the changeless spiritual conditions that make persecution an enduring reality in the Christian experience.

This book will consist of three sections. Section 1 examines cultural attitudes toward Christianity, with the actions and approach of the Sanhedrin serving as the first model for persecution. Section 2 draws a line in the sand, noting essentials where Christians must be in agreement if they are to keep their Christianity intact. Section 3 elaborates on two crucial issues in contemporary Christianity—belief in the Bible and the trend toward belief in an unbiblical Jesus—and how to respond to each of them.

The goal of this book is not to change America. Only God can do that. This book was written with a view toward changing the manner in which we as Christ's followers respond to modern trends within our culture. I believe that attitudes we face are becoming more antagonistic because of our efforts to capitulate. In many ways the church has begun to look too much like the prevailing culture and is therefore unable to provide a viable alternative.

This fact has been disguised by the success of the megachurch. Many Christians believe that the existence of churches that boast memberships in the thousands is evidence of effective Christian outreach in our culture. Unfortunately, a closer look tells quite another story. In her book *Worship Evangelism*, Sally Morgenthaler examines the truth behind the trends and uncovers some disturbing realities. For example, church attendance has steadily declined in the United States over the past two decades. From 1991 to 1994, church attendance in America dropped from 49 percent to 42 percent.[1] The consequence of declining attendance has been the death of an estimated one hundred thousand congregations in the decade of the 1990s.[2] But what about the megachurch phenomenon? Megachurch attendance figures are large but deceiving. Eighty percent of the growth in the average megachurch is the result of the transfer of members from one place to another. Moms and dads are looking for someplace bigger, someplace with "facilities for the children" and all the bells and whistles. One congregation in Houston even has a McDonald's franchise *in the church!* Hence, people pack up and leave the small church and head for the giant congregation with the new buildings and the menu full of options.

There is nothing inherently wrong with a large church. I am simply saying that the existence of large congregations does not negate the fact that church attendance in America is on the decline. We are not winning our culture. In fact, it can be argued that our culture is winning us. I cannot tell you how often I receive calls from pastors who are trying to invite me to their church but have trouble finding a viable date because of football or baseball or band!

Much of this capitulation to secular culture's demands stems from the fact that over the years Christianity in America has been more American than Christian. I am not speaking of a decline in morality here, though there is ample evidence that the lack of biblical morality in the modern American church has hampered our ability to communicate the gospel to our culture in a winsome and effective manner. I am talking about something deeper, something more fundamental. I am talking about one's *worldview*. The fact is that *what* we believe determines *how* we behave. My goal is not to tell Christians what to do but to challenge what we believe. Currently, much of what we believe is shaped by our culture, and, unfortunately, much of what our culture believes on a fundamental level is diametrically opposed to biblical truth.

How belief should impact behavior is a question facing missionaries around the world. Many people hear the gospel and are more than willing to respond, but they do not always see the need to alter cultural practices that contradict their new faith. Imagine trying to convince a person steeped in the traditions of ancestral worship that he or she must dismantle an altar that has been in the family for generations! Or what does one do with a people-group whose former religion allowed the taking of multiple wives?

Our own questions may be somewhat different, but American Christianity is not immune to these difficulties. Anyone who has been to a business meeting in a Baptist church (I can talk about Baptists because I am one) will tell you that much of what goes on is a lot more American than it is Christian. In fact, the first time I ever saw *Robert's Rules of Order* used outside of an academic setting was in a church business meeting. When I asked one of the deacons about the absence of such rules in the Bible, he looked at me like I was speaking in tongues! I was not trying to be coy. I didn't grow up in church and didn't know how things worked. All I knew were the principles I had gleaned from the Scriptures, and when I saw procedures that didn't fit, I wanted clarification.

I understand that there are different expressions of Christianity in different cultures. Contextualization is essential for the growth and expansion of the church. But there is a difference between contextualization and compromise. Using goat's milk for communion in a culture that has never heard of wine or grapes is contextualization; sacrificing the goat is compromise. Having a Saturday night service because we have run out of room in all four Sunday services is contextualization; having a Saturday night service to accommodate and/or appease people who are "too busy" on Sunday is compromise.

Peter and John did not change for the sake of their culture. They simply lived for Christ and preached the gospel. They did not adapt Christianity to the culture, nor did they seek to adapt the culture to Christianity. Their goal was to transform individuals by proclaiming the gospel and making disciples. They realized that there were two incongruent kingdoms at work in the world, and they did not fight that reality. Rather, they embraced it.

I am not suggesting that believers completely withdraw from the culture. That would not be a biblical position. I am, however, suggesting that we be *in* the world but not *of* the world. The sad truth is that many of us live lives that have been so affected by our culture that we feel completely at home in a place that was not made for us and, quite honestly, does not welcome us. Many of us can't remember the last time our Christian convictions cost us something.

This past soccer season, the league in which my son and daughter were playing had to make up two games due to rain (the price of living in Houston). The consensus in the league was that Sunday was the only available day, so the makeup games were scheduled for Sunday afternoon. My family and I sat down to discuss the matter, but no discussion was really necessary. There was no way we were going to participate. Sunday is the Lord's Day, and playing youth soccer games on Sunday makes a definite statement about the priorities in a community.

Interestingly, the most flak from our decision came not from the irreligious people involved but from Christians! "You can go to church, then run home and change for the game," one man said. One of my children's coaches added, "I'd be glad to pick them up if there is somewhere you have to be." Nobody seemed to get it. We weren't making a decision based on the hectic nature of our Sunday schedule, nor was it a question of our adhering to a legalistic requirement handed down from our denomination. It was a matter of principle. Sunday is more than just another day. Youth sports leagues are great, but they are not sacred; Sunday is!

Again, I do not believe that there is a legalistic requirement not to play games on a Sunday. Nor do I believe that the policeman, fireman, or airline mechanic who goes in to work on Sunday is out of the will of God. I do, however, think that there is a huge difference between someone whose job requires working on Sunday and a soccer league that just doesn't care.

This culture-accommodating attitude may not seem like much, but the implications are huge. There has been a gradual shift among many Christians in our culture—so much so that it has become increasingly difficult to distinguish between those who follow Christ and those who do not. The frog-in-the-kettle analogy is apropos to our situation. Place a frog in a kettle of boiling water, and he will fight to escape, or so the story goes. That same frog, if placed in tepid water, will not notice a gradual increase in temperature; he will simply lie still and be boiled alive. Friends, some of us are in hot water, and we don't recognize the danger.

Churches often exercise forms of government that mirror secular governing bodies instead of the New Testament model. Young Christians get married and tell God how many children they are going to permit him to give them and when he is allowed to start. Christians walk in and out of marriages, citing not Scripture but "irreconcilable differences" as the grounds for their divorce. In many larger churches, the new criteria for pastors is modeled after corporate CEO's instead of the descriptions in such Bible passages as 1 Timothy 3, Titus 1, and 1 Peter 5. The temperature is rising, and if we don't jump out before it boils, we will find ourselves following in the footsteps of our brethren in the United Kingdom and other parts of Europe. At one time there, churches stood as monuments of the reviving presence of God, but in many places they now serve as museums—or even pubs.

Have we forgotten who we are? We need to remember we are "a chosen race, a royal priesthood, a holy nation, a people for God's own possession, so that you may proclaim the excellencies of Him who has called you out of darkness into His marvelous light" (1 Peter 2:9).

The apostles were not embraced by their culture; a society at odds with their message hated them and put them to death. A central cultural governing body was the Sanhedrin, a sort of Jewish supreme court or senate that handled religious disputes and matters regarding local jurisdiction. It consisted of an austere group of seventy men, all overseen by the high priest. The court's existence was an example of the Romans' efforts to keep peace by allowing conquered nations to govern themselves under Roman supervision. The healing of the lame beggar, about which Peter and John were questioned, would have fallen squarely within their jurisdiction and was precisely the type of matter to which they would have given their full attention (see Acts 3:1–10).

In fact, it had been the Sanhedrin that had eventually brought charges against Jesus due to the furor over the miracles he performed and the audacious claims he made. They had feared the Roman response. Concerning the raising of Lazarus, for example, Robert Gundry notes: "The Sanhedrin was afraid that by reviving His popularity this latest miracle of Jesus would bring about a messianic revolt that would bring down harsh Roman reprisals."[3] How, then, did the Sanhedrin respond when Jesus' followers began to do and teach the same things they had feared from Jesus? "Now as they observed the confidence of Peter and John and understood that they were uneducated and untrained men, they were amazed, and began to recognize them as having been with Jesus" (Acts 4:13).

And so the interrogation began. This opening statement sets the tone for the balance of the apostles' encounter with the Sanhedrin. Everything that follows flows from the assumption that Peter and John were, in their understanding, not well-enough educated to speak and act as they had done.

A common mistake when reading this text is to interpret the phrase "uneducated and untrained men" to mean that Peter and John were illiterate country bumpkins. To do so would require quite a stretch. For instance, we would have to believe that these two illiterates gave us the Gospel of John, the three Epistles of John, Revelation, and 1 and 2 Peter. In addition, we would have to believe that these two men did not receive the training that was part of a Jewish boy's life in the first century. When all of their contemporaries were memorizing the Pentateuch or Torah, they would have to have somehow managed to skip out to go fishing.

A better explanation is that the governing council recognized the message Peter and John were preaching and, more specifically, the similarities between their words and those of Jesus. Hence the description in verse 13, "They were amazed and began to recognize them as having been with Jesus." In fact, the term "uneducated" (*agrammatoi*) was not exclusively used to refer to someone who was illiterate; it was also a description for those who had not been "trained in Greek rhetoric or public speaking as the priestly aristocracy would be."[4] The term may also suggest that they had not been trained by an officially recognized rabbi.

Thus, Peter and John were not being accused of stupidity or illiteracy but of nonconformity. It is as though the Sanhedrin were saying, "There is a way in which a teacher should conduct himself, and the two of you do not fit that mold. In fact, it's worse—you sound as though Rabbi Jesus taught you!" All of these accusations came while a man who was once lame now frolicked in the streets.

John Calvin noted this irony when he commented: "Here we see an evil conscience. Devoid of reason, they launched an all-out attack. So Luke first mentions their astonishment to show how against God they were. They saw God's work in the healing of this man, and yet they wickedly opposed him. They acknowledged that Peter and John were unschooled, ordinary men and that something more than boldness was with them. So they were astonished, whether they liked it or not. But they were so impudent that they opposed the truth like tyrants."[5]

The ruling council was disconcerted by the manner in which Peter and John conducted themselves and constructed their defense. The priests and elders simply could not believe that men without their own level of training could be unafraid when brought before them to be questioned or that they could deliver such concise, cogent arguments.

The Sanhedrin's reaction is similar to the indictment leveled against contemporary followers of Christ who do not fit into the mold of modern-day thinkers. Those of us who insist on believing and doing what the Bible says find ourselves labeled as narrow-minded, unthinking, untrained, and uneducated babblers. We sound as though we have been following Jesus. And that, in many circles, is unthinkable.

And what is our greatest sin? We actually think we know the truth! We actually believe that we have met God. To top it off, we don't believe that our encounter happened in some New Age, esoteric fashion; we actually believe that God has revealed himself and made himself knowable to everyone. We believe that this revelation is available to us in the Bible and that this revelation is the standard of all truth.

Truth Wars

Truth is under attack in modern American culture. Rare is the person who believes that there are facts that correspond with reality (truths) and that those facts are true for all people in all places and at all times. Common, however, is the man or woman who believes that all religions are the same (religious relativism), that tolerance is the ultimate virtue, and that there is no absolute truth (philosophical pluralism).

Innocuous as these beliefs may seem, they are dangerous. They lead down a path filled with peril. If all religions are the same, then no religion is true. Moreover, if we believe there are no absolute truths, and all truths are equally valid, this will ultimately lead us to nihilism wherein all ideas lose their value. Ultimately, the only thing that will matter is who has sufficient power to exercise his or her will.

Imagine that you woke up today and saw this news flash: "All bills in American currency declared equal." No longer is the $100 bill more valuable than the $1 bill. Under the new system the only thing that matters is who has the most bills of any kind. Thus, a person holding a hundred $1 bills now has the same purchasing power as a person holding a hundred $100 bills. The only question would be, "How many bills do you have?" Of course this would never fly. People would revolt and demand that the value of their bills be recognized.

While this scenario is highly unlikely, it is precisely what has happened in the marketplace of ideas. No longer does the value or validity of one's ideas matter. All ideas are declared equal, or at least equally valid. Furthermore, it is very important that those with $100 ideas not attempt to argue against the validity of $1 ideas. Those who question are labeled intolerant, for the act of discerning truth undermines the very core of relativism.

These beliefs form the foundation upon which current thinking and philosophy are built. However, they are not being taught as classroom subjects. Teachers don't stand up and say, "Today we are going to learn religious relativism." In fact, many people are not aware of the presuppositions underlying their belief systems. These ideas have become so ingrained in today's thinking that they simply persist without being questioned. Many people regard relativism, tolerance, and pluralism as basic courtesy.

The University Lays a Foundation

Anyone wishing to understand the cause of the rapid spread of this post-Christian mind-set must examine our colleges and universities. One of my first religion professors made this concept very clear to me. I had just written my first paper in my Old Testament class, and he called me into his office to discuss some of the content. He told me that I was not being "academic" enough. I relied too much on the Bible, he said. Later in the semester he called me in after a statement I had made on a test that alluded to Jesus as the ultimate fulfillment and manifestation of one of the principles we were covering. This time, he was not as patient with me. The conversation occurred over thirteen years ago, but I will never forget it. He said, "You are not here to be an evangelist." He went on to say that perhaps I was not suited for religious studies.

I started preaching during the summer before my junior year in college. Eventually, I transferred from prestigious liberal arts college to a Christian school in order to better prepare for my vocation. I progressed rapidly and eventually gained entry into Theta Alpha Kappa, a national honor society for theology students. At one of our banquets, a professor with whom I had become friends introduced me to the man who would be our speaker for the evening. We walked over and I stuck out my hand and said hello, and our guest almost choked! It was my old professor from Rice, the one who had told me that I was not well suited for religious studies. As my mother would say, "You could have bought him for a quarter!"

He was astonished! He honestly thought that an "evangelist" like me who believed that Jesus is the only way to God and that the Bible is the Word of God could never be a successful student of theology. I have thought of that man many times. I thought of that professor when I went off to seminary, and the recollection motivated me to achieve. I thought of him when I had the privilege of gathering with a group of religious leaders from around the country to advise Governor George W. Bush on religious issues as he pursued the presidency of the United States. I thought of him when my family and I were on the plane to England, and when I studied in the postgraduate program at the University of Oxford. I also thought of him when I was hooded at my graduation ceremony at Southeastern Seminary upon earning my doctorate. And yes, he is on my mind as I write this book. Not just him, but what he represents—the notion that anyone who does not buy into the ideals of religious relativism, the new tolerance, and philosophical pluralism has checked his or her brain at the door and is essentially "uneducated and untrained."

My motivation to succeed did not come from a desire to prove my professor wrong. On the contrary, my motivation came from the fact that in many ways he was right. He spoke for the culture at large. He represents the "informed intellectuals" and "academics" in our culture. He was not a voice crying in the wilderness. He was one of the cornerstones of an academic program at one of America's top universities. His answers to religious questions would be considered learned and progressive to many people. One can find attitudes similar to his at many of our nation's top secular schools and even at some "Christian" universities and seminaries.

In his book *The Real Jesus*, Luke Timothy Johnson reflects on this trend that has become the norm in theological education.

He states: "First-year students, who often come to seminary with deeply conservative convictions concerning the inspiration and inerrancy of the Scripture, are exposed at once to the 'shock therapy' of the historical critical method. They are told by eminent professors, often in tones of scarcely contained glee, that everything they ever believed is wrong, and that to be part of this new academic environment they must accept the 'historical critical view' of the Bible."[6]

Johnson's assessment rings true in far too many instances. I am reminded of a conversation I had with a friend of mine who attended a seminary that fit Johnson's analysis. At one of his lowest points during his second year of seminary, my friend said, "I'm not God, and I can't judge a person's heart, but if I had to guess, I would say that no more than one or two of the professors I have had are saved." Again, this was during his second year in seminary!

I realize that my comments may sound harsh, but many examples support both Johnson's assessment and my friend's experience. Bishop John Shelby Spong, retired from the Episcopal Church, spoke at the William Beldon Noble Lectures given at Harvard University Divinity School in March 2000, and his most recent book began its life there. Spong set out to identify the key components of traditional theology with which he disagrees. In the opening pages of his book he states, "I do not believe that Jesus could or did in any literal way raise the dead, overcome a medically diagnosed paralysis, or restore sight to a person born blind or to one in whom the ability to see had been physically destroyed."[7]

He continues:

> I do not believe that Jesus entered this world by the miracle of a virgin birth or that virgin births occur anywhere except in mythology. I do not believe that a literal star guided literal wise men to bring Jesus gifts or that literal angels sang to hillside shepherds to

announce his birth. I do not believe that Jesus was born in Bethlehem or that he fled into Egypt to escape the wrath of King Herod. . . . I do not believe that the experience Christians celebrate at Easter was the physical resuscitation of the three-days-dead body of Jesus, nor do I believe that anyone literally talked with Jesus after the resurrection moment, gave him food, touched his resurrected flesh, or walked in any physical manner with his risen body.[8]

These beliefs are understandable in light of Spong's view of the Bible: "I do not believe that the Bible is the 'word of God' in any literal sense. I do not regard it as the primary source of divine revelation. I do not believe that God dictated it or even inspired its production in its entirety. I see the Bible as a human book mixing the profound wisdom of sages through the centuries with the limitations of human perceptions of reality at a particular time in human history."[9]

While Spong is not a tenured professor, he had enough academic clout to lecture extensively at Harvard Divinity School, and he cannot be overlooked. Lest you think these are the rantings of some maniacal ivory-tower theologian out on the fringe, think again. Bishop Spong's last book was a *New York Times* best seller! Views such as his are not limited to Harvard or the Ivy League schools. They are increasingly mainstream.

Perhaps a more poignant example is Marcus Borg, the Hundere Distinguished Professor of Religion and Culture at Oregon State University. Speaking of his previous (read "orthodox") beliefs concerning Jesus, he writes: "I believed in that Jesus without difficulty and without effort. I now understand why it was so easy: I received this image of Jesus in what I have since learned to call the state of precritical naiveté—that childhood state in which we take for granted that whatever the significant authority figures in our lives tell us to be true is indeed true."[10]

According to Borg, his seminary experience eventually liberated him from this "precritical naiveté" that characterized his former faith. He writes:

> There I learned that the image of Jesus from my childhood—the popular image of Jesus as the divine savior who knew himself to be the Son of God and who offered up his life for the sins of the world—was not historically true. That, I learned was not what the historical Jesus was like. . . . I learned that the Gospels are neither divine documents nor straightforward historical records. They are not divine products inspired directly by God, whose contents therefore are to be believed (as I had thought prior to this). Nor are they eyewitness accounts written by people who had accompanied Jesus and simply sought to report what they had seen and heard.[11]

If Borg's comments sound similar to Spong's, it is no coincidence. Both men's statements stem from the same philosophical presuppositions. Unfortunately, these statements are typical of scores of professors of religion and theology throughout the United States and the world. And many of these theologians disseminate their views in seminaries designed to train the pastors and professors of tomorrow.

This is not to say that the seminary is a bad place. On the contrary, I am disturbed by the increasing level of disdain for theological education among evangelicals, some of which stems from the presence of professors like Borg, but much of which stems from antiintellectualism in the church. However, I am also disturbed by the fact that seminaries and divinity schools are often judged by the degree to which they embrace the aforementioned views.

When people learn that I have degrees from two conservative Southern Baptist seminaries, they tend to receive the information with a yawn. However, when they discover that I also did postgraduate work at Oxford, their eyes light up, and I almost expect them to kneel down before me and exclaim, "We're not worthy!" Ironically, Marcus Borg is an Oxford product. Most of what I encountered there epitomized liberal, inclusivist, postmodern, and deconstructionist theology.

"So why did you go?" I can't tell you how many times I have been asked that question. The answer is simple: "Because I could." OK, maybe it's not that simple. First, I saw an opportunity to stretch myself. I knew I would be in enemy territory and that my views would be tested. Second, I wanted to see the other side up close. I wanted to hear the arguments being made from the ground up by people who sincerely held these beliefs. Third—and this is the subject for another book—as a black man, I am sick of the stigma that affirmative action has attached to my accomplishments. It is constantly assumed by some that every academic achievement in my life is at least to some degree the product of quotas or set-asides.

I tell people I went to Rice, and they assume, "You must have played football," and I did. But that is not the point. Other football players from Rice—whose complexion is not as dark as mine—usually get a different response. They hear, "You must be pretty smart." Granted, I have received my share of those comments, but they have been few. I saw Oxford as an opportunity to place myself in an environment free of the stigma of quotas, set-asides and lowered standards for black students. I saw it as an opportunity to remove even the perception that I was being judged by anything other than the "content of my character." Affirmative action may seem out of place in this discussion, but it is not. Affirmative action in the name of diversity is at center stage in the pluralism/relativism discussion, as I will demonstrate in chapter 2.

I spend a great deal of time on college campuses, and some of the most common questions I face have to do with students desiring to defend their faith to their professors. I can't tell you

how many times students have asked me, "How can I respectfully engage a professor who insists on railing against
Christianity?" Another popular question is, "What documenta-
tion can I use to refute evolution?" In recent days, in light of all
of the statements about the "peaceful" nature of Islam, another
question is, "Where can I go to get balanced information on the
history and theology of Islam?"

These questions arise out of an adversarial environment
where Christianity in many cases has been deemed intolerant
and narrow. The university campus is the front line in the battle
for truth. It is here that the ideals and philosophies that charac-
terize the age of relativism are shaped, packaged, and perpetu-
ated. It is here that mature men and women challenge and often
disrupt the flimsy foundations upon which the ideals of young
students are built. Regrettably, the concepts with which the student's ideals are replaced are not born out of sound academic
research and clear logic; instead, they are birthed out of
unfounded philosophical presuppositions. What's worse, the
university is not alone. The culture at large provides many allies
in this battle for the student's beliefs, not the least of which are
our legal system and the media.

The Legal System Joins the Battle

I do not mean to suggest that the American legal system is
out to get Christians. That is simply not true. However, there are
several legal issues that I believe shed light on the current post-
Christian cultural climate. Each of these issues has remained at
the forefront of recent legal battles, and none of them shows
any signs of losing momentum anytime soon. While the following is not an exhaustive list, I think it will suffice to make the
point.

The Separation of Church and State

The frequency with which this term is used causes some to marvel when they discover that the phrase "separation of church and state" cannot be found in the Constitution. That's right, it's not there! Thomas Jefferson coined the phrase in a letter he wrote to the Baptist Association in Danbury, Connecticut, in an effort to assure them that the rumors they had heard about the establishment of a state church were false. His letter reads as follows:

> Gentlemen,
>
> The affectionate sentiments of esteem and approbation which you are so good as to express towards me on behalf of the Danbury Baptist Association give me the highest satisfaction. . . . Believing with you that religion is a matter which lies solely between man and his God; that he owes account to none other for his faith or his worship; that the legislative powers of government reach actions only and not opinions, I contemplate with sovereign reverence that act of the whole American people which declared that their legislature should "make no law respecting an establishment of religion or prohibiting the free exercise thereof," thus building a wall of separation between Church and State. Adhering to this expression of the supreme will of the nation in behalf of the rights of conscience, I shall see with sincere satisfaction the progress of those sentiments which tend to restore to man all his natural rights, convinced he has no natural right in opposition to his social duties. I reciprocate your kind prayers for the protection and blessing of the common Father and Creator of man, and tender you for yourselves and your religious association assurances of my high respect and esteem.[12]

Jefferson's sentiments become clearer when viewed in light of his many remarks and writings on the subject. In his second inaugural address, for example, he stated that in matters of religion, "its free exercise is placed by the constitution independent of the powers of the general [federal] government." David Barton, a leading advocate for the appropriate rendering of the First Amendment as it relates to Christianity in American culture, believes that "Jefferson had committed himself as President to pursuing the purpose of the First Amendment: preventing the 'establishment of a particular form of Christianity' by the Episcopalians, Congregationalists, or any other denomination."[13]

The First Amendment, which many cite as the source of the doctrine of the separation of church and state, reads in part, "Congress shall make no law respecting an establishment of religion, or prohibiting the free exercise thereof." These simple words are a far cry from the interpretation often expressed and discussed today. Due to a simple misreading or misapplication of the words of Thomas Jefferson *written in a private letter*, this issue has reached a point of crisis. Barton's conclusion puts a fine enough point on the matter:

> Therefore, if Jefferson's letter is to be used today,
> let its context be clearly given—as in previous years.
> Furthermore, earlier courts had always viewed
> Jefferson's Danbury letter for just what it was: a per-
> sonal, private letter to a specific group. There is proba-
> bly no other instance in America's history where words
> spoken by a single individual in a private letter—
> words clearly divorced from their context—have
> become the sole authorization for a national policy.
> Finally, Jefferson's Danbury letter should never be
> invoked as a stand-alone document. A proper analysis
> of Jefferson's views must include his numerous other
> statements on the First Amendment.[14]

Jefferson's own words, encapsulated on the Jefferson Memorial in Washington, DC, summarize his thought: "I have sworn upon the altar of God, eternal hostility against every form of tyranny over the mind of man." Jefferson's goal was not to keep religion out of the halls of government; he wanted to keep government out of the halls of religion.

Hate Crimes Legislation

Whenever I raise this issue, people look at me like I am from the moon. "You are an African-American. How can you be suspicious of hate crimes legislation?" one man asked. After explaining to him that I am not an African-American (or any other kind of hyphenated quasi-American), I went on to raise several questions about hate crimes legislation that continually give me pause.

Who defines hate?

Hate is a difficult concept to quantify. Does a person who steals from a grocery store do so because he or she hates the store? Does the drug addict destroy his or her body out of self-hatred? How about the serial killer who targets strangers? Can one hate a stranger? These are just a few of the questions that must be addressed if we are to define hate. Currently, hate seems to be defined by preferred minority groups who believe a priori that those who commit crimes against members of their group must do so out of hate. I say "preferred minority groups" because hate crimes do not span the gamut of minority groups. Laotians, for example, are a racial and ethnic minority in America, but they are not protected by hate crimes legislation. Do we actually believe that no one hates Laotians? No! They simply do not have the political clout or a large enough voting block to exert the political pressure necessary to achieve preferred minority status. Therefore, they do not get to participate in defining hate in our society.

Who does hate crimes legislation protect?

Do the DC-area snipers qualify for hate-crimes prosecution since there is evidence that they did what they did out of hatred for America? Of course, the answer to this question is no. There are only a few groups that are included in hate-crimes statutes. Most legislation targets crimes committed against individuals or groups because of their race, gender, sexual preference, national origin (actual or perceived), and religion.

What about the Packers fan who beats up the Bears fan because he hates the Bears? Isn't that a hate crime? What about the person who hates Swedes, Brits, Norwegians, Canadians, or Australians? Why is it that killing a black or Hispanic person is a hate crime, but killing an Australian is just a crime? Isn't all murder motivated by hate? In fact, it could be argued that every violent crime is a crime of hate. But that is not the way the law works.

Who does hate crimes legislation punish?

On the morning of November 6, 2002, two black students at the University of Alabama woke up to find racial epithets written on their dorm-room doors. The unspeakably vile words were accompanied by a stick figure drawing of a lynching. The entire campus was in an uproar. Eventually, civil rights activists joined the fray, calling for public condemnation of the actions by the university administration and a commitment to pursue both state and federal hate crimes charges against the perpetrators.

Why then was there no outrage when the perpetrators were not prosecuted? Why was there no appearance by black leaders protesting the fact that no arrests were made and no state or federal hate crime charges were filed? Why are most people completely unaware of the events that followed the capture of the criminals? Why? Because they were black! That's right, three black students committed these hate crimes against two black fellow students.

Had three white students been caught committing these crimes, the NAACP, the ACLU, Jesse Jackson, and Al Sharpton would have been on every national news program demanding justice! No sentence would have been sufficient, no apology from the university would have been satisfactory. However, the three black culprits will likely receive no more than a slap on the wrists, and that will bring no outrage.

The event's significance devolved from another reminder of the ever-present racism in our culture to a prank pulled by immature, unthinking college students who should not have their futures ruined by a momentary lack of judgment. The irony is palpable. The newspaper headline, "Students at Ole Miss torment black students with racial epithets and get away with it," sounds like one from the 1950s or 1960s. The crucial difference is that in the past someone would have been shouting about injustice from the rooftops.

What is the ultimate goal of hate crimes legislation?

I wish that the goal of hate crimes legislation was to end hate, but it is not. In fact, not only is that not the goal of hate crimes legislation, but it is not the goal of legislation in general. Legislation serves only to punish crimes, not to end them. Legislation against theft, burglary, assault, and other crimes does not end those crimes; it merely grants society the means by which those who commit the crimes are punished. Hate crimes legislation, though, is unique in that it does not seek to punish people for what they do but for what they feel and think.

For example, a person who paints a Nazi symbol on a Jewish temple is already guilty of vandalism. A person who burns down a black church is already guilty of arson, and a man who kills another man because of his race, national origin, or sexual preference is already guilty of murder. Each of these people would be punished for his crimes regardless of whether we had hate crimes statutes. The difference the new laws make is that now we are authorized to crawl inside the perpetrators' heads to determine whether they have animosity toward a "preferred minority." If so, we punish them *more*.

I fear hate crimes legislation may eventually make it a crime to preach sermons from parts of the Bible that address homosexuality, abortion, and other hot-button issues. Ultimately, this legislation can do nothing about the crimes themselves, only about the perceived source of these crimes, the so-called hate-speech. No doubt some of the statements in this book, such as salvation through Jesus alone, would be considered hate-speech by some!

The Ten Commandments

One of the fiercest debates in our land in recent years has been over the issue of whether it is appropriate for copies of the Ten Commandments to hang in public places such as schools and courtrooms. The posting of the Ten Commandments is so prominent in the United States that there is actually a copy in the Supreme Court. They are viewed as a foundation upon which the very concept of law is built.

Opposition to the posting of the Ten Commandments is usually based on the aforementioned separation of church and state myth. The Anti-Defamation League, for example, explains their organization's opposition as follows: "Opposition to state-sponsored posting of the Ten Commandments does not arise out of hostility to the timeless values conveyed in Exodus 20:1–17. Rather, it arises out of a profound respect for the diversity of religions in America today—those that embrace Biblical law and those that derive their ethics and values from other texts. By adhering to the principle of separation of church and state we best fulfill the Constitution's legacy of religious liberty for all Americans."[15]

That's right. It matters not that the Ten Commandments serve as the backdrop of our nation's legal heritage—the possibility that they may offend atheists is what is important.

2
CULTURAL IDEALS ABOUT TRUTH

The philosophy that governs present-day American culture is founded upon at least three basic ideals: religious relativism, tolerance, and philosophical pluralism. These ideals are so widely accepted as true that they are rarely challenged. Any attempt to address our culture must analyze and respond to these three ideals.

Myth 1: All religions are the same.

According to the myth of religious relativism, we all worship the same god; we just refer to him (or her) by different titles. Religious relativism is willing to overlook even the most glaring contradictions between religions in an effort to preserve unity and peace. For instance, following this thought process would lead one to proclaim that Judaism and Satanism are not mutually exclusive but are, in fact, both expressions of worship to the same deity.

A classic illustration used to argue this point is that of the elephant and the blind men. Four blind men come upon an elephant. The first man touches the elephant's tail and exclaims, "It is long, thin, and sturdy; it must be a rope." The second man touches the elephant's trunk and declares, "It is long, thick, and warm; it must be a snake." The third man examines the elephant's leg, then he surmises, "It is thick, sturdy, long, and appears to be planted in the ground; it is obviously a tree." The fourth man reaches up and explores the elephant's vast body. After feeling around on one side, he proclaims, "You are all wrong. It is extremely large, sturdy, and firmly in place; this is obviously some sort of building or shelter."

This illustration makes what religious relativists consider a crucial point: Everyone has a limited perspective, and none of us has all of the answers. While this point is valid, it does not require a leap in logic that many professors employ in order to argue that this illustrates the fact that none of us can know the truth. Besides, the fact that the blind men are wrong does not negate the fact that there is an elephant there. In the same way, the fact that many people are wrong about God does not negate his existence. Unfortunately, this conclusion is often lost on those to whom this lie is fed.

My initial exposure to religious relativism occurred during a religion course in 1989. The title of the course was "Christian/Jewish Dialogue." A religion professor facilitated the course, but the primary lecturers were a Jewish rabbi and a Methodist minister. The entire course was a long lesson in political correctness and religious relativism. Our lecturers put it this way: "It is as though God is on the top of a mountain and all of us are merely climbing up different sides, yet headed for the same destination." I had no idea that this course was meant to indoctrinate my classmates and me, but that was precisely the plan. Any attempt by a student to identify differences was met with swift rebuke.

I later encountered the same ideology as a postgraduate student at Oxford University. At one point an expert in the field of interfaith witness told me that it was both wrong and unnecessary for a Christian to take his or her faith to people who practice other religions because they are "worshipping the same

God, merely doing it in different ways." The interesting thing about both of these incidents is that in both cases the perpetrators, one of them a pastor, were part of an academic program designed to teach the Christian faith!

How have so many people come to this conclusion?

The roots of this myth can be traced to a philosophy called *naturalism*. Naturalism is the belief that *nature* (the material and the laws that govern its existence) is all there is. There is no force beyond nature, no supernatural or metaphysical reality beyond us. Thus, God is merely a figment of our imagination. Phillip Johnson offers this definition: "According to naturalism, what is ultimately real is nature, which consists of the fundamental particles that make up what we call matter and energy, together with the natural laws that govern how those particles behave."[1]

Unfortunately, naturalism's presuppositions dominate the thinking of our day. Johnson calls scientific naturalism and its related liberal rationalism the "established religious philosophy of late-twentieth [and I would add early twenty-first] century America."[2] But what does naturalism have to do with religious relativism? It's quite simple: If there is no supernatural world (and thus no God), and if all the religions of the world actually find their source in the minds of men, then they are all equally useless. Hence, it makes no difference which religion one chooses; they are all, in the words of Governor Jesse Ventura, "crutches" created by weak-minded people who need help coping with the cruel world.

In this kind of philosophical environment religious relativism makes complete sense. If there is no supernatural realm (no God), then anyone who believes in such a being is merely constructing his or her own reality. Ultimately, then, religious belief is no more than self-delusion. Therefore, one person's self-delusion about the existence of a supernatural being is no different from anyone else's. It's all a farce! Johnson summarizes naturalism's view of God as follows: "To put it another way, nature is a permanently closed system of material causes and effects that can never be influenced by anything outside of itself—by God, for example. To speak of something as 'supernatural' is therefore to imply that it is imaginary, and belief in powerful imaginary entities is known as superstition."[3]

This ideological position often leads to a pragmatic stance on religion that is best represented by the all-too-common statement, "As long as you find something that works for you. . . ." I wish I had a dollar for every time I've heard that one. It sounds tolerant and open-minded, but the question is, Does it really make sense? What if what works for me is flying planes into buildings in the name of my god? There are serious practical and philosophical problems with this view, which we will expose in turn.

Myth 1 Exposed: Religious relativism is illogical.

The problem with religious relativism is twofold. First, it violates the law of noncontradiction, which states that a thing cannot be both A and non-A at the same time and in the same way. Let me state that in layperson's language. The law of noncontradiction says that something cannot be dairy and nondairy, fattening and nonfattening, or biased and unbiased at the same time and in the same way.

Consider this illustration: Imagine that you have come to the end of this book and immediately begin to call all of your friends to tell them to run out and buy a copy. You call a buddy in New York and tell him you just finished a book by a great new author named Voddie Baucham. He gasps! "Did you say Voddie Baucham?" He asks in astonishment. "Yes, Voddie Baucham," you reply. He responds enthusiastically, "You gotta be kiddin' me. You just read a book by *the* Voddie Baucham?" (Just go with me on this part.) Again, you calmly respond, "Yes, Voddie Baucham." To which your friend replies, "Voddie Baucham! The little white guy from Brooklyn?" Now in order to understand how ridiculous this is, you would need to know that I am over six feet three inches tall and well over . . . well, I weigh a lot, and I am a Texan by choice, who was born and raised in Los Angeles, California.

The way I see it, there are two possible responses to your friend's question: "No, that is not the Voddie Baucham who wrote this book; you must be talking about another guy." Or the second alternative, "Well, that's your interpretation of who he is!" No one would view this second response as valid, or would they? It is this second response that sums up the fallacy of religious relativism. Two groups can talk about God in terms that are mutually exclusive and still conclude that they are talking about the same being.

The fact is, however, that only one Voddie Baucham is the author of this book. If he does not fit the aforementioned description, he is actually someone else. In the same way, only one God is the Author, Creator, and Sustainer of the universe. We cannot all be right—especially when we disagree on essential issues.

Therefore, to say that Islam or any other religion that states that Jesus is merely a prophet and that he is not divine, and that Christianity, which believes that Jesus is God incarnate, are equally valid is nonsense! Both positions cannot be true simultaneously, but this conclusion is precisely the position of religious relativism. Satanism and Judaism are equally valid. Hinduism and atheism are both true. And the list goes on. To believe such drivel is to commit intellectual suicide.

Myth 1 Exposed: Religious relativism is offensive.

In addition to being illogical, religious relativism offends adherents to all religions. To equate the views of the Muslim and the Christian is to insult them both. To liken the Satanist to the Jew is the height of distaste. I talked to a Muslim friend during the days following September 11, and his sentiment was exactly the same as mine. He was offended by the fact that people were equating Islam with Christianity. He and I are friends, but we do not pretend that we worship the same God. We both know that is simply not true.

Anyone who watched the news in late 2001 or early 2002 was inundated with the idea that Muslims and Christians worship the same God. Many persons interviewed, from Islamic scholars to Christian clergy to the president of the United States, have either made this statement or strongly alluded to it. In fact, it has been rare to see anyone offering a contrasting opinion. I do not believe that their unanimity is the result of a media conspiracy. No, it is something much more sinister. It is the natural result of our culture's inundation with religious relativism. This statement keeps recurring because most people believe it. The real question, however, is not what most people believe but what is true.

In the aftermath of the bombings of the Pentagon and the World Trade Center towers, news anchor Peter Jennings aired a special on Islam. The format was unique and contrived. The studio was filled with junior high and high school students. Some were Muslims, but most of them identified themselves as Christians or Jews.

Jennings asked his young audience to tell him what they knew about the religion of Islam. As one would expect, they knew very little. Their answers were astonishing. One young man said he thought Muslims ate people. Many of the students admitted that they had no Muslim friends and that they did not know where they had received their information.

After several minutes of this informal discussion, a Muslim cleric was brought in to "set the record straight." "It is amazing how misinformed people are about Islam," he said, shaking his head in disbelief. He then went on to describe Islam as a misunderstood religion of peace. Although I disagree with his assessment of Islam, it was his next statement that elevated my blood pressure a few counts. He said, "The truth is we all worship the same God." Amazing! Muslims and Christians worship the same God? How can that be? How can a group of people who consider it *shirk* (blasphemy) to assert the divinity of Christ or the doctrine of the Trinity claim to worship the same God as those who believe that God revealed himself to humankind in the person of Jesus Christ? Isn't this illogical? Of course it is, unless you buy into certain cultural myths about truth.

Myth 1 Exposed: Religious relativism ignores the facts.

The greatest threat to religious relativism is an exclusivist view of religion. To an exclusivist, God revealed himself in a very specific way, and only those who respond to that revelation properly can hope to be in right relationship with him. Exclusivism leaves no room for multiple roads to God; there is only one way. Christianity and Islam, for example, are both exclusivist religions.

Jesus taught that he was "the way and the truth and the life" and that no one could come to the Father except through him (John 14:6). The Bible also teaches, "There is salvation in no one else; for there is no other name under heaven that has been given among men by which we must be saved" (Acts 4:12). Again Jesus said, "This is eternal life, that they may know You, the only true God, and Jesus Christ whom You have sent" (John 17:3). Christianity is a faith system that leaves no room for religious relativism.

According to the Bible, faith in Jesus Christ is the only way to salvation. Hence, any faith system that teaches any other means of salvation, whether works, reincarnation, universalism, martyrdom, or any other process, would be considered incorrect from the Christian perspective. Such exclusivism is unthinkable to religious relativists, even those who call themselves Christians. It presents quite a quandary for those who wish to consider all religions as equally valid. How does one acknowledge Christianity as one valid alternative among many when Christianity refuses to be categorized as such? The answer is quite simple—paint a new picture of Christianity.

In addition to the special on Islam described above, Peter Jennings also emceed a series called *The Search for the Historical Jesus*. In what was supposed to be a balanced report, Jennings paraded one "expert" after another before the camera. The only problem was that almost all of them were members of a notorious liberal, quasi-academic think tank called the Jesus Seminar.

The Jesus Seminar has publicly denied the virgin birth, the miracles of Jesus, any sayings of Jesus having to do with his divinity or exclusivity, the resurrection, and of course the second coming. In short, these people deny virtually *every* essential doctrine of the Christian faith! Why, then, are they chosen as spokespeople for Christianity? Because theirs is the only brand of Christianity that will fit into a culture of religious relativism!

Getting rid of Christianity is not a realistic option. Instead, our culture has chosen to redefine the faith using "academic experts," thereby classifying the exclusivist Christian who actually believes the Bible as a narrow-minded, uninformed, uneducated, and insensitive bigot. The only problem is that the so-called experts don't have a single shred of evidence to support their claims. Their claims are not based on hard data but on presuppositions and leaps in logic.

Myth 2: Tolerance is the greatest virtue.

The catalyst for this approach to religion is the modern definition of tolerance. The goal of religious relativism is not to be logical, but to be tolerant. Tolerance is the virtue that trumps all others in our culture. It is more important to be tolerant than it is to be honest, loyal, or trustworthy. Moreover, the tolerance to which I am referring is not the tolerance of old. Today's version is what Josh McDowell calls the "the new tolerance."[4]

Tolerance once meant putting up with someone or something in spite of the fact that one did not like or agree with the idea or the person. Today, however, tolerance has morphed into a big hairy monster that demands we not only put up with but even embrace and celebrate the views and practices of others. Furthermore, the new tolerance demands that we value the views and practices of others to the degree that we value our own.

We attribute to Voltaire the statement, "I may disagree with what you have to say, but I shall defend to the death your right to say it." This sentiment is a thing of the past. Today such ideas are considered out of touch and even intolerant. We are no longer allowed to disagree. This is an untenable position. This is the type of thinking that prompted G. K. Chesterton to exclaim, "Tolerance is the virtue of a man without conviction."

Today tolerance has topped the charts, so to speak, in the area of virtues. Nowadays, the worst thing that can be said about a person is that he or she is intolerant. I recently had a conversation with a couple in an airport that typified our culture's view on tolerance. We sat next to one another and began to share airport small talk. Eventually, we got around to the "Where are you from?" portion of the conversation. "We are from Southern California," the woman said. "Really," I replied, "I grew up in Los Angeles." They both smiled and asked, "Where do you live now?" "Houston, Texas," I replied. The woman let out an audible gasp. "Texas!" she exclaimed, making no attempt to hide her disgust. "They are so *intolerant* there!" "What do you mean?" I asked. Her answer would have been funny had it not been so sad. She said, "I hear they hate black people and Jews. They don't want women to have abortions, and they don't want evolution in their schools."

Interestingly, the closest they had come to Texas was flying over it in a Boeing 737. Furthermore, they ignored the fact that I am both black and a Texan and feel right at home. However, the sentiment they expressed is all too common—all people must be allowed to do and believe whatever they want and anyone who disagrees with that in any way is a bad person. That's right; no longer can we agree to disagree and be civil. The mere act of disagreeing is now considered uncivil.

Please don't miss this point. Persons who do not agree with one of the fundamental principles by which present-day culture operates are not simply wrong—they are intolerant. In other words, their entire character has been impugned. Listen to what this statement actually says: "You *are* intolerant." Not your position, not your view, but you! Granted, there are some subscribers to the tolerance creed who choose not to take the issue that far, but the fact remains that tolerance is no longer just an issue; it is a virtue to be prized above all others.

The Myth Exposed: Tolerance is itself intolerant.

The problem with the new tolerance is that it is intolerant! The present view sees tolerance as it is defined by religious relativists as an essential element in all public affairs. Thus, intolerance, in the words of one public school principal, "must not be tolerated." What exactly does one call the act of not tolerating intolerance? Could it be . . . intolerance? Why did the woman from California view Texans as intolerant because they allegedly oppose abortion? Why aren't people who support abortion called intolerant for not accepting the pro-life position? And what about the issue of evolution in schools? Why aren't evolutionists labeled as intolerant for refusing to give equal time to creationism? The inconsistency is mind-boggling!

Tolerance claims to consider all views and practices as equals. However, a closer look reveals that this is simply not the case. For example, tolerant people are expected to view all religions as equally valid, with all roads leading to God. Hence, anyone who does not adopt this view is deemed undesirable. This means that Christianity and Islam, among others, are examples of religions that violate the virtue of tolerance and would thus be considered inferior to more tolerant religions. If this is the case, then the proponents of tolerance value Christianity and Islam less than other religions. But remember, the essence of tolerance is supposed to be that of valuing all religions equally. There is a logical problem here!

Consider this statement: "We value all trees equally, but the trees that drop leaves in the backyard have to go because they are too much of an inconvenience." I find it amazing that people do not realize the ineptitude of this position. Imagine *Consumer Reports* being attacked because it rates one automobile over another. Why is it that consumers' ratings can rank cars and trucks and appliances based on their performance and their ability to deliver on their claims and never be considered "intolerant" toward the inferior products? Why? Because the key component of modern tolerance is people's freedom to believe and behave as they choose without being subjected to the ire of those who disagree.

Southern Baptists saw a great example of the inconsistency of the new tolerance at the 2002 Southern Baptist Convention, when homosexual activists stood outside picketing because of what they considered intolerance on the part of the Baptists. The convention was not emphasizing any particular gay issues or taking any monumental positions on the subject. The problem, according to the picketers, was that homosexuals weren't properly represented in the SBC.

It seems that homosexual activists desire to see the SBC change its stance, not only on issues like gay marriage but also on homosexuals in church and convention leadership. In their minds this is the tolerant thing to do. Thus, it is deemed acceptable to demand that an entire denomination deny the teachings of the Bible upon which it was founded, thus undermining the essence of its faith, in order to accommodate the views and practices of a vocal political group. How can this be?

Am I the only one who sees the irony here? The homosexual activists, demanding tolerance from others, are themselves being intolerant! They refuse to accept people who pattern their lives after the clear instruction offered in the Bible. However, there were no cameras outside with reporters covering the intolerance of the activists. Imagine, though, what it would be like if a bunch of angry men and women who called themselves Christians had gathered carrying signs that demanded changes in the beliefs and structures of a homosexual organization. I can just see the headline: "Homophobic fundamentalist Christians disrupt gay rights rally in a monumental display of intolerance." *Good Morning America* would have a parade of guests on the show the next day bemoaning the fact that people are not allowed to do whatever they want in the privacy of their own bedrooms.

This double standard has become so common that few people seem to recognize the hypocrisy. No one seems to notice that students can go to public schools with T-shirts that promote violent television shows like *WWE Smackdown* and *Ultimate Fighting,* while others are asked to turn their shirts inside out because they have a cross on them. No one seems to notice that students are allowed to write reports on the religious beliefs and practices of the ancient Greeks and Native Americans, but the Bible has virtually been banned from inclusion in such activities. In short, no one seems to notice that the new tolerance is extremely intolerant when it comes to Christianity. But that's OK because, after all, like Peter and John in Acts 4, we are the "untrained and uneducated men" of our day.

Myth 3: There are no absolutes.

The denial of absolute truth is a hallmark of modern thinking. While there are many sources of this ideology, the key to understanding them all is to understand a broader philosophy called *postmodernism.* While this is not a book on postmodernism, it is necessary to offer more than a passing comment on the subject. It is impossible to understand the post-Christian worldview without a basic understanding of postmodernism.

I recently received a phone call from a colleague in the ministry who was about to accept a new church position. He called me to discuss the great news and to ask a question. Although he was excited about the church he was going to serve, he was confused about his new job. He was being hired as the "pastor of postmodern ministries."

This new title sounded exciting, but it was a bit confusing. "Isn't postmodernism a bad thing?" he asked. I went on to explain that a common mistake in much of the teaching on postmodernism is that many people want to reduce it to generational issues. You have boomers, busters, Gen Xers, and postmoderns. Hence, postmodernism is reduced to the mind-set of children born after a certain year, usually designated as 1984.

While it may be harmless to use the term *postmodernism* in that way, it does not help us address the real issue. Our problem is not generational: it is philosophical. Most Americans are postmodern in their thinking. It doesn't matter if they are five or fifty! Thus, it is important to know that the term *postmodernism* was coined to describe the philosophy that grew out of modernism, and in order to understand postmodernism, it is essential that we understand the ideology that it supplanted. We begin, therefore, with a discussion of *modernism*, the worldview that postmodernism is said to have replaced.

Modernism

It is largely agreed that the roots of modernism lie in the Renaissance and in the scientific revolution of the seventeenth century.[5] Advances in architecture, art, and science established a sense of unparalleled optimism. Diseases were being cured; natural laws were being discovered; new technology was constantly being introduced; and all problems suddenly appeared to be solvable.[6] Moreover, human reason appeared to be the source of these immanent solutions.

The rationalism of the era known as modernism led to a belief in the ultimate and unmatched ability of human reason to discover ultimate truth. The premise and preeminence of reason was said to be unassailable during this era.[7] Modernity, according to David Harvey, was an "extraordinary intellectual effort on the part of Enlightenment thinkers to develop objective science, universal morality and law, and autonomous art according to their inner logic."[8] He goes on to point out that modernism was for the most part "a secular movement that sought the demystification and desacralization of knowledge and social organization in order to liberate human beings from their chains."[9]

Rationalism and a sense of humanistic optimism characterized the modern era.[10] The Catechism left the classroom and the study of religion replaced the study of theology. Only what could be proven scientifically was deemed worthy of being taught as fact; all else was considered "dogma."[11] The search for objective truth through humanistic rationalism, without any spiritual or moral goal, threatened to become a mere instrument to subjugate others.[12]

Postmodernism: A Reaction to Modernism

Simply put, *postmodernism* is a term used to describe the philosophical response to the Enlightenment period.[13] Thomas Oden put it simply: "If modernity is a period characterized by a worldview which is now concluding, then whatever it is that comes next in time can plausibly be called postmodernity.[14] While this response took many forms, the driving force behind each of them seems to be the desire to counter the hegemony of modernism. It is important to note that since postmodernism is a reaction, there are no real tenets of the movement, as such; there are merely trends.

David Bosch goes to great lengths to point out that the use of the term *postmodern* is not a statement of value. The term, according to Bosch, is merely a "heuristic" notion.[15] His emphasis is on the fact that *postmodernism* is simply a word used to describe a new paradigm or reaction. The response to modernism, he argues, has occurred in seven major areas: The expansion of rationality, the demise of the "subject-object" scheme, rediscovery of the teleological dimension, the challenge to progress thinking, and a fiduciary framework. Whereas this list may be an oversimplification, it will serve as a foundation upon which to build the following argument. In plain terms, Bosch argues that in the postmodern perspective, language is deemed incapable of achieving absolute accuracy, nature cannot be viewed mechanically, universal design must be viewed from the perspective of purpose, and facts cannot be distinguished from values.[16]

Pluralism: The Definitive Expression of Postmodernism

Those offering a critique of postmodernism often use the term interchangeably with pluralism. In fact, many of the works cited in this chapter include the words *pluralism* or *pluralistic* in their titles. Thus, it becomes necessary to understand both concepts. There are three types of pluralism: empirical, cherished, and philosophical.[17] Each variety of pluralism has unique implications to which we must pay close attention.

Empirical pluralism is a mere statement of fact. As international travel becomes easier and more affordable and as people continue to migrate toward jobs, opportunities, and freedom, more people migrate to the world's large cities.[18] This reality has created an environment wherein cultures and religions once separated by thousands of miles now coexist in the same neighborhood. America, as an example, is now "the largest Jewish, Irish and Swedish nation in the world."[19]

Empirical pluralism has led to a dangerous kind of syncretism that must be addressed in contemporary missiology. The blend of religions and cultures has created in some cases a blending of theology. No longer can one make assumptions about the theological understanding of individuals within certain geographical boundaries. Pluralism is a matter of fact. For instance, listen to the demographic configuration of this Texas family, who are close friends of ours: The husband is from Lebanon, and the wife was born in Cuba. They are both Eastern Orthodox Christians, and their sons go to Arabic school. That is empirical pluralism.

Cherished pluralism is merely empirical pluralism with the added element of approval.[20] Carson argues that empirical pluralism has become "a value in itself, even a priority."[21] The existence of different beliefs and ideals is seen as inherently good. Diversity is at a premium in cherished pluralism. In fact, lack of diversity, whether in business, media, art, entertainment, education, or elsewhere, is viewed as evil and "exclusivist."[22]

We see this phenomenon today in many arenas. For instance, the increased priority placed on diversity on our college campuses is one result of cherished pluralism. Minority students (read "blacks, Hispanics and women") are routinely accepted in top-tier universities with grades and test scores that are considerably lower than those of other students against whom they compete for open positions. A prime example of this practice has been seen in the recent national controversy over the University of Michigan's admissions policy. Students were given points for their accomplishments, such as GPA, SAT scores, and extracurricular activities. Students with one hundred or more points usually had no problem getting in. The controversy arose over the fact that students were given twenty points for being black, as compared to only twelve points for a perfect sixteen hundred on the SAT!

The pull of diversity is strong. The U of M has all but stated, "Diversity trumps academics." It could not be clearer. The idea of a student body with a specific number of minorities is seen as more important than packing the campus with the brightest minds available.

This idea has also invaded the church. I cannot tell you how many times I get calls from pastors asking me to come preach at their churches with the added caveat, "We have a lot of African-Americans in our community, and we really want to reach them," as if having a black preacher in one's pulpit is actually going to bring the local black community running down the aisles to join their church. Let me be clear: I have nothing against my white brethren attempting to reach anyone and everyone within their church's sphere of influence. I am, however, increasingly sensing that the goal is not saving souls but presenting a more diverse image to the community.

Promise Keepers is one organization that has gone out of its way recently to appeal to diverse ethnic groups. Earlier, the organization was drawing tens of thousands of men, but with only sparse representation from nonwhites. Following orders from the group's headquarters, Promise Keepers' planners began engaging a list of speakers that shortly began to look like roll call at the United Nations. First came an African-American, then a Hispanic, then a Native American, followed by an Asian, and all in the name of diversity.

Far be it from me to say that adding these speakers was not a noble or even a godly endeavor. However, I think it needs to be pointed out that diversity is not a biblical mandate. Nor is it realistic. For starters, who decides when something is diverse enough? I live in Houston, one of the most ethnically diverse cities in the United States. There are more than seventy foreign consulates in this city. One hundred or more languages are spoken here. Are pastors in Houston to believe that unless they have at least sixty nationalities represented in their congregations, in the same percentages as they occur in the city at large, that they have failed to fulfill the r calling? Or can we say that a predominantly white church with a spattering of black and Hispanic members represents true diversity in such a diverse city? Again, how can one quantify *true* diversity? Beyond that, what would this true diversity prove?

The fact is that there is a Houston statistic that is far more important to our Christian mission than the number of nationalities represented. That number is 2,500,000. That's right— there are some two and a half million unchurched people in the Greater Houston area. Pastors are beating themselves up over the fact that they don't see enough diversity in the pews while more people than make up the populations of 95 percent of America's cities are on the outside of the kingdom of God! Meanwhile, we worry that congregations in our area are comprised of 90 percent of one race or another. Again, we see the massive pull of cherished pluralism.

Philosophical pluralism is summed up in the belief that any particular ideology's or religion's "claim to be intrinsically superior to another one is *necessarily* wrong."[23] The only absolute creed is that of pluralism.[24] Here, one moves beyond both empirical and cherished pluralism to a position that ultimately denies the existence, or at least the attainability, of objective truth. Thus, Leslie Newbigin states, "The fact of plurality . . . must be distinguished from the ideology of pluralism."[25] Whereas the impact of empirical pluralism on ore's worldview may be benign, adopting philosophical pluralism represents a definite shift.

The seminal influence in philosophical pluralism is the deconstructionism of Jacques Derrida.[26] This French philosopher set the standard wher it came to deconstruction. Essentially, he argued that texts do not communicate meaning. Meaning, according to Derrida, is always subjective; the meaning of a text has more to do with culture, perspective, and endless possibility and progressive alteration of language than with correspondence to any objective truth. Thus, deconstructionism ultimately denies either the existence or the attainability of absolute truth.

While classifying deconstructionism with these terms over-simplifies what is a highly complicated system, it also demonstrates the main thrust of Derrida's argument. Derrida's principles originally referred to the art and science of hermeneutics, but the application of them in many instances has been cultural relativism, and relativism has led to the pre-eminence of pluralism as a valued belief in today's culture.

The Myth Exposed: Philosophical pluralism is inconsistent.

The greatest problem with philosophical pluralism is its inconsistency. The pluralist argues that there are no absolutes. The problem with this assertion is that it is an absolute statement. One may as well say, "There are absolutely no absolutes." This is preposterous. It is a clear example of the "self-excepting fallacy" at work—claiming that something is true for everyone but oneself. This is precisely the problem with postmodern culture. We are told to hold on to an ideology that states that it is wrong to hold on to ideologies. If that sounds confusing, it should!

I have been trying unsuccessfully for some time now to convince God to let me conduct an experiment. What, you ask, do you want to do? It is quite simple. I want to find someone committed to philosophical pluralism and engage that person in debate. The moment he says that there are no absolutes, I punch him in the mouth!

I know what you are thinking, but follow me for a moment. If the person is committed to philosophical pluralism, then he or she should get up and say absolutely nothing. If he does, I will simply exclaim, "Violence toward you is necessary for my well-being." Of course the debater's response would be, "That's not right." To which I will respond, "What's right for you is not necessarily right for me."

At this point the postmodern thinker will have a choice. If he persists and wishes to have me punished, he will have to deny postmodern philosophy. Or he can hold firmly to philosophical pluralism and take a chance on being struck again.

Of course, I would never do such a thing, but I am sure you get the idea. Pluralists say they don't believe in absolutes, but they are not rushing to empty the jails, nor are they willing to allow someone to violate or mistreat them without proper legal recourse. Both of these actions would be necessary to practice true philosophical pluralism.

The pluralist's response to this argument is that humans must make laws in order for society to survive. In addressing this issue, C. S. Lewis pointed out that society's survival would have to be established as an absolute necessity before such an assertion could be made. Lewis faced this issue directly in a series of lectures called "The Case for Christianity." He argued that the belief that there are no moral absolutes is betrayed by the desire in all people to be treated fairly or properly and by their complaints when they are not. Lewis states:

> Now what interests me about these remarks is that the man who makes them isn't just saying that the other man's behavior doesn't happen to please him. He is appealing to some kind of standard of behavior he expects the other man to know about. And the other man very seldom replies, "To hell with your standard." Nearly always he tries to make out that what he has been doing doesn't really go against the standard, or that if it does, there is some special excuse.[27] . . . It looks, in fact, very much as if both parties had in mind some kind of Law or Rule of fair play or decent behavior or morality or whatever you like to call it, about which they really agreed. And they have.[28]

We have all seen it. Someone who is wronged lashes out against the other person for violating some unspoken rule or law about fair play or basic decency. Lewis argues, and I agree, that this behavior is evidence of an innate sense of right and wrong present within all of us. Inevitably, some would argue that the presence of evil in the world or disagreements between cultures about this "innate" sense would serve as proof against its existence. Lewis used the reality of World War II, the context in which he gave his lectures, to refute this argument:

> They called it Law of Nature because they thought every one knew it by nature and didn't need to be taught it. They didn't mean, of course, that you might-n't find an odd individual here and there who didn't know it, just as you find a few people who are color-blind or have no ear for a tune. But taking the race as a whole, they thought that the human idea of decent behavior was obvious to everyone. And I believe they were right. If they weren't, then all the things we say about the war are nonsense. What is the sense in say-ing the enemy are in the wrong unless Right is a real thing which the Germans at bottom know as well as we do and ought to practice? If they had no notion of what we mean by right, then, though we might still have to fight them, we could no more blame them for that than for the color of their hair.[29]

Not surprisingly, there are those in our day who are so com-mitted to philosophical pluralism that they argue that the actions of Nazi Germany were not wrong! The Nazis, they say, were just doing what was right for them at the time. One would hope that an argument against such a ridiculous ideology would be unnecessary. Unfortunately, that hope is far from real-ity. Philosophical pluralism is alive and well, and its proponents can be found in the highest levels of government, education, law, and even the church. Failure to address this issue would be an egregious error.

3
NEUTRALITY IS
NOT AN OPTION

The apostles' encounter with the Sanhedrin in Acts 4:15–16 is quite revealing: "So they ordered them to withdraw from the Sanhedrin and then conferred together. 'What are we going to do with these men?' they asked. 'Everybody living in Jerusalem knows they have done an outstanding miracle, and we cannot deny it'" (NIV).

Sending the accused out of the council was a common occurrence. During this time Peter and John would have been placed under guard outside the meeting hall. The text provides no information as to what, if anything, they said to one another, but they had to remember what had happened to Jesus when brought before that same council! They had gained attention because of their miracles and teachings—so had Jesus. They were branded as religious and political outsiders—so was Jesus. They were guilty of no crime—and neither was Jesus.

Inside, the members of the Sanhedrin must also have remembered Jesus. Their trepidation came from two directions. First, the popularity of Peter and John threatened their positions and authority. They must have thought that if these men continued to cause such a stir they would certainly gather followers. Second, if this band of rebels gathered too much momentum, they would eventually gain the attention of the Roman govern-ment. This kind of attention could be disastrous. According to the edict of *religio licita*, any religion that was older than the Roman Empire and practiced by the subjects of the empire prior to their conquest could continue to be practiced.[1] Thus, the Jews had the right to practice their religion, continue their sacrifices, and govern themselves in religious matters. However, this new sect would not be protected under the edict. Not only would the adherents of the new group be persecuted, but since they were also Jews, the persecution could spread to other Jews, as well.

Something had to be done! They could not simply let these men go. News of this event would certainly spread, as would the notoriety of the one in whose name it had been performed. Jesus had been crucified in order to squelch this movement, but here it was again threatening the status quo. Because all the people were praising God for the miracle, they decided to take no legal action, but they issued a strong warning.

American Christians have been fortunate. We live in one of the few societies in the history of Christianity that has not per-secuted the followers of Jesus. We know nothing of the suffering of our brothers and sisters in southern Sudan who are being beaten, enslaved, chased from burning churches, or even killed by their predominantly Muslim enemies in the northern part of the country. We know nothing of the secrecy that must be main-tained by our brothers and sisters in China, who must meet in underground churches in order to escape the ire of the Communist government and their anti-Christian policies. Most of us are oblivious to the torment of believers in Muslim coun-tries, who find themselves targets of discrimination, violence, and even murder. We can't imagine the pain of a Coptic Christian woman in Egypt whose fourteen-year-old daughter was kidnapped from her home and raped by Muslim men, who then informed her that her daughter had been converted to Islam and that she would not see her again.

These are just a few of the painful realities with which the followers of Christ around the world live on a daily basis. I am not suggesting that American Christians will face this kind of persecution; we may not. What I am suggesting, however, is that the idea of being accepted by a culture whose ideology is fundamentally at odds with biblical Christianity is not realistic. Currently, the only persecution we have seen has been mild, at its worst.

Nevertheless, there are signs that biblical Christianity is losing favor in our society. One sign is the portrayal of Christians on television and in the movies. I am not one of those guys who blame TV for all the ills of society. While I admit that there are times when members of the media should be held accountable for the poison they peddle, I believe that there are far more instances when they are merely reflecting the ideology of the age. In either case, a simple examination of the portrayal of Christians on TV and in the movies provides insight into either the attempts of the powers-that-be, or their reflection of the age in which we live.

Luke Timothy Johnson, commenting on this issue, makes this observation:

> The coverage of religion in this country reveals the weirdness of the situation insofar as the media exercises its "ideal identity," it tends to treat religion gingerly and negatively. The working press, after all, continues to self-select its members according to the mold of such cultural despisers as Samuel Clemens and H. L. Mencken, for whom religion was of interest primarily for its unerring ability to cultivate charlatans and fleece the gullible. This, more than a conspiracy of "liberal bias" . . . tends to make the coverage of religion an afterthought when it is thought of at all.[2]

Johnson is by no means a "right-wing fundamentalist"; he is a first-rate scholar at what is considered by many to be a theologically moderate institution. Johnson's book is not about the media; it is about the Jesus Seminar. His comments concerning the media are directly related to the level of attention focused on this relatively small group due to its ability and desire to exploit the natural tendencies of many media outlets.

Let's take a closer look at what I am getting at. When I was a kid, I loved to watch reruns of MASH. I don't know if it was the military themes, the irreverent humor, the underlying moral to each show, or the fact that I got to stay up late. Nevertheless, I couldn't wait to hear the familiar theme song and watch that helicopter bring in the wounded at the opening scene.

One of my favorite MASH characters was Father Mulcahy. He was the jovial, somewhat naïve priest who often served as the straight man for Hawkeye's jokes. I was not a Christian at the time, but I remember thinking fondly of Father Mulcahy. Unfortunately, as I look over the current landscape, I don't see many lovable religious characters on television anymore. It is as though the current cultural climate will not tolerate a positive religious persona.

Father Mulcahy is a character of television's past. Today's portrayals of religious people in television shows and the movies seem to fall into several common categories. Each program seems to rehash the same old stereotypes. It seems that the portrayal of a neutral or positive Christian character has been forbidden by the scriptwriters. Of course, I don't believe that. I actually believe something far worse! I believe that the portrayal of religious people, particularly Christians, is not the result of some sinister plot to misrepresent and vilify Christianity—it is simply a symptom of the shift in thinking which views Christianity as intolerant and ignorant. Hence, what we see is a portrayal of Christians that is shaded by the lenses of religious relativism, tolerance, and philosophical pluralism.

In his book *Bias,* Bernard Goldberg points out that Christians are one of the only groups in America upon which the media can heap insults without fear of reprisals.[3] That is not to say that there is never a positive portrayal of Christians or Christianity in the media. Occasionally a film or news story does portray Christians in a positive light, but these occurrences are not the norm. You are much more likely to see Christians depicted in, shall we say, less than flattering ways.

TV and Movie Portrayals of Christians— a Wide Array of Stereotypes

Moviemakers love to target priests. They find it easy, in part, because a priest's uniform allows the director to present an easily identifiable type. Put a man in a priest's collar, and you don't have to explain who or what he is. Priests have been receiving inordinate attention in films and on television, partly because of bad press they have attracted over recent years. Still another reason Catholic priests seem to be the representatives for religion may be that the myriad rituals of the Catholic Church just seem more "religious" than other faiths. Whatever the reasons, priests are easy targets, but the stereotyping crosses both Catholics and Protestant clergy and all varieties of Christianity from liturgical to charismatic traditions.

The Drunken Lush

The drunken priest has been portrayed so many times that it is hard to pick an example. There are countless films and television shows that depict priests as men who spend their entire day getting drunk. Who could forget the drunken friar who played opposite Kevin Costner in *Robin Hood*? He was a jolly old plump fellow who couldn't wait for his next drink of ale.

The Tortured Man

Another popular portrayal is the priest whose lust is so obvious that it is embarrassing. He meets a girl and suddenly has to battle between his vow of celibacy (frowned upon by our culture) and his sexual desire for the woman (celebrated by our culture). Whether he chooses his vocation or his libido, the message is clear—uncontrolled sexuality is to be preferred over unreasonable and unrealistic commitment to God.

As I was writing this chapter I took the time to go to the movies. I was away preaching in North Carolina for a few days, and the worship team and I went to see the new summer blockbuster *Signs*. I loved the Alfred Hitchcock style in which the film was directed. However, my companions, who knew I was working on this chapter, kept glancing over at me every time the main character, Graham Hess (Mel Gibson), would do something that exemplified the tortured-man stereotype—and reinforcement of that stereotype occurred often.

Graham is a former priest (his denomination is never mentioned, but he was probably Episcopal) who lost his faith when his wife was killed in a tragic accident. He promptly left the priesthood and eventually vowed, "I'm not going to waste one more minute of my life on prayer." The movie is filled with moments where his abandonment of the Christian faith takes center stage.

Graham's faith was restored by the *circumstances*, not by the God who restored his Son. The idea here is that his faith was not in God, but in the signs or events.

The ideology represented here fits squarely within the scope of our postmodern, existential culture. "If it works for you, do it!" That's the battle cry that can be heard beneath the sympathetic portrayal of this tortured man who simply needs some evidence upon which to base his faith. One wonders, though, what will happen when Graham Hess experiences another tragedy.

The Spiritual Doormat

Horror films are filled with examples of this guy! He is the one who holds up the cross in front of the vampire only to be mocked because of his lack of belief or who cringes in the face of the ghost or demon who is about to crush him. The purpose of this character is to demonstrate the impotence and irrelevance of religion.

The prototypical spiritual doormat has to be the highly educated, somewhat spiritual priest in *The Exorcist*, Father Karras. At one point, when questioned by the mother of the possessed girl, he says he does not believe in demon possession because of the "stuff [he] learned at Harvard."

The Lapsed Catholic

This stereotype is so common that no examples are necessary. How many times have we seen the character who wears the crucifix, goes to mass, makes the sign of the cross when things get tough and has absolutely no other religious convictions! There is also the recurring appearance of the character who, during a moment of revealing dialogue, admits that he or she "went to Catholic school."

Of course, no discussion of the lapsed Catholic would be complete without at least a mention of those stereotypical Italian mobsters who kill for sport but always baptize their infant children and who believe in adultery but not divorce. From *The Godfather* to *The Sopranos*, this character is a common type.

The Rigid Nun

This is another overdone stereotype. In fact, it is so exaggerated that Whoopi Goldberg made millions laugh in her movie *Sister Act* because she loosened up several of the straitlaced sisters. Who can forget these classic prudish women as they learned to cut loose and boogie? What made this movie so funny was not just the comedic timing, the classic clichés, or the awkward manner in which the nuns participated in the musical numbers; what ultimately made this movie funny was its reinforcement of a prevailing stereotype.

The Child Molester

Since the recent onslaught of cases involving pedophile priests has rocked the Roman Catholic Church, TV shows on the subject have proliferated. Weekly TV crime dramas from *Law & Order* to *The Practice* have exploited the issue's potential for attracting viewers. A rash of made-for-TV movies has also explored the topic.

I am not suggesting that pedophilia should be swept under the rug. On the contrary, I would like to see a thorough treatment of all of the issues involved. For example, what are the ramifications of practicing celibacy? I am just pointing out that when priests do something good, the writers in TV Land are not falling over one another to produce the latest twist on the story for their weekly drama.

The Slick Televangelist

How many times have you turned on the TV and heard the familiar cadence of the televangelist? Before you look up, you know exactly what you are going to see: a slicked-back, greasy-haired, out-of-date, white-suit-wearing, fast-talking, country con artist whose evil deeds will be exposed by the end of the episode.

In addition, his followers will be portrayed as uneducated, ignorant, naïve, gullible, well-meaning people who are simply too stupid to see through his lies. If they are allowed to speak, they will say embarrassing, stereotypical things about the "good Lord" and faith.

The Thoughtful Liberal

A recent episode of *Law & Order* (It's no secret that I am a crime drama enthusiast!) explored the issue of abortion clinic killings. The villain was a fundamentalist Christian who had killed a doctor because of his religious beliefs (more about this stereotype later). However, the twist was that his hatred of abortionists was ignited not by his sincerely held religious convictions but by an overbearing father and a girlfriend who had aborted their child in college.

In this case the girlfriend represented the thoughtful liberal. She, too, had grown up in a strict religious home but quickly realized that her parent's teachings and, consequently, that of her strict Christian religion were unreasonable and outdated. She "saw the light" and aborted the unwanted child. She decided that she didn't need to take her religion too far. She was portrayed as the ill-fated victim who was fortunate enough to live in a land where she had "the right to choose."

This episode is a classic example of an extreme view being used to justify a particular moral position and to squelch all legitimate debate. The argument against abortion was never voiced. The only people who held the pro-life position were the antisocial murderers whose parents and pastors had forced them into an extremist group. The message was clear. There are two kinds of people in the world: those who protect a woman's right to abort her child, and the freaks who are too dense or misguided to agree with them.

The Invisible "Extra"

One of the most ironic moments in the history of film is the scene in *The Godfather* when Michael Corleone, accompanied by several of his henchmen, is attending the baptism of his infant son. This is just one of many instances where the "religious" person, in this case a priest, appears merely as a movie "extra," performing what is, in the grand scheme of the film, a meaningless task.

Another common scene is that of the robed pastor performing a wedding ceremony. My favorite version of this occurs in the daytime soaps. Typically the story will feature a suspense-filled buildup to an elaborate wedding. The bride is always dressed in a stunning white gown, and the groom looks like he just jumped out of GQ. Everyone in the room is smiling with that familiar "this is the most beautiful thing in the history of the world" look on their faces. The nameless minister begins that familiar ceremony, and the fairy tale is complete, for about a dozen episodes.

The irony is that the couple being married is almost certain to have expressed absolutely no religious commitment whatsoever throughout the rest of the series, but when it comes time for the "I dos," enter the preacher. Marriage is presented in films and on TV as a completely secular undertaking, but there must be a big, traditional wedding. Characters can go through a string of husbands or wives, but every time they get married, they go through the empty ritual of a traditional "Christian" wedding along with the vows that they have made and broken six or seven times before.

While what results is not necessarily a negative portrayal of Christians, it is definitely a negative portrayal of Christianity. The message is that Christianity is essentially a collection of meaningless rituals performed by irrelevant people. There is also the idea that the Christian ceremony is fine, but please, no Christian marriages, and certainly no Christian courtships! Purity is simply not allowed.

The Radical Activist

The movie *Contact* is Carl Sagan's swan song. *Contact*'s answer to the question of the existence of life on other planets is an affirmative one. However, *Contact* is not just a typical sci-fi flick. Rather, it is intended to be a true-to-life account. The aliens don't have large heads and flying saucers; they communicate through higher mathematics and respond to television signals broadcast into space.

There are several instances where religion is referenced in the film. The undertone is that religion is the opiate of the masses. Everyone except the intelligent scientists believes in God. One religious character, the love interest of the main character, is portrayed as a cross between the tortured man and the thoughtful liberal. However, the most poignant portrayal is that of an activist who blows up a spacecraft designed by the aliens.

At first this man seems to be merely a stereooypical (read: liberal) religious figure who preaches against the "voices from the sky" and their potential to lure us away from God. Later, though, he takes action, donning a jumpsuit and wiring the flight deck with an explosive device. The juxtaposition of the radical activist and the thoughtful liberal is an obvious ploy. The point is clear: There is life out there, and its existence disproves the foolish beliefs of unreasonable religious people who insist on believing in things like the Bible. However, there is hope for those who don't take their religion too seriously.

The Regular Guy

Several years ago many American Christians began to rave about a great new "Christian" show. It was touted as a wonderful family-oriented sitcom with distinct Christian themes. In fact, the father in this TV family was a minister. The show was called *Seventh Heaven.* I watched the show for several months, and I must say I was not impressed.

The father is the epitome of the regular guy. His beliefs are not biblical; they are simply tolerant and very pluralistic. In fact, one entire episode is dedicated to his youngest son's quest for the real meaning of Christmas. His quest takes him to a mosque, a synagogue, and a Catholic church. Eventually, he settles on a pluralistic stance that greatly pleases his father.

Lately the show has deteriorated to the point that virtually every episode centers on the sexual escapades of the older children. The father is as confused and frustrated as any other father, and his advice sounds no different. He is just a regular guy who happens to wear a robe to work on Sundays.

The show's producers would perhaps argue that they are trying to present a positive picture. The problem is that their efforts flow from a worldview that considers biblical values obsolete and that those who hold and practice them are pathetic. Hence, they present a family with morality that directly reflects the cultural norm, headed by a father who just happens to punch the clock at a church where he occasionally gives "good talks."

TV and Movie Portrayals of Black Christians— the Stereotyping Continues

I was born in 1969, which gives me the privilege of having grown up during what some consider the Golden Age of the portrayal of blacks on television. As a child of the 70s who came of age in the 80s, I remember shows like *Good Times*, *The Jeffersons*, *What's Happening*, and, of course, the greatest of them all, *The Cosby Show*.

These programs had elements of satire and did not always show the best side of black people or families. Nevertheless, they were a long way from the portrayals of old. They were about more than the pimp, the pusher, and the prostitute. These shows were about black families—not perfect but not flat and stereotypical either. Like most blacks, I enjoyed and was proud of these shows. Unfortunately, I cannot say the same about the way films written and produced by blacks portray black men in general, and particularly black preachers. Ironically, the worst cases are often seen in so-called "black" films.

The Cultural Performer

I gave up on awards shows several years ago. I realized that watching the *Grammy Awards* or the *American Music Awards* only served to infuriate me and remind me how out of touch I am with the current music scene. I got sick of watching scantily clad performers win awards for songs that glorified promiscuity, violence, and perversion, and then adding insult to injury by thanking God!

I also began to notice a more subtle issue. Gospel music was thrown into the mix. Gospel music was added as an award category and gospel performers were added to the program, usually at the end. Why? Was it because gospel music had gained the respect of music executives? Or could it have been a result of a massive influx of Christian artists who pushed from the inside? No, I don't think either of these scenarios is the cause. The answer is actually a bit more cynical.

Traditional black gospel music is viewed as a fading cultural art. Gospel artists are the keepers of the gate, so to speak. They are the ones who are keeping the traditions of yesterday alive. Honoring and remembering gospel music is simply a means of acknowledging its contribution to other types of music, such as soul or R & B, and its place in a significant segment of black culture. The issue is not one of including a certain *perspective* but one of including a certain *performance.*

To the secular music world, the gospel artist, with her booming, soulful voice, her hands raised toward heaven, and her foot stomping out the rhythm of a repetitive, pulsating tune, is in many ways no different from the Native American rain dancer. Both are viewed as interesting characters from our history that got people through difficult times by providing something to believe in.

How else can you explain why the same group of people would stand and clap their hands and stomp their feet to a gospel tune after having applauded Nelly's performance of *"It's*

Gettin' Hot in Here"? The irony is palpable! Even more ironic, Victoria's Secret employed a gospel-style choir for their grand finale in their prime-time television broadcast during which models walked the runway in some of the most revealing lingerie imaginable. I cannot imagine what choir would agree to provide the background music for a striptease, but that is practically what happened.

Victoria's Secret's marketing team was not attempting to create a worshipful atmosphere but a lustful one. They were not trying to draw attention to God; they were trying to draw attention to . . . you know what they were trying to draw attention to. Their choice in music had nothing to do with their respect for the choral traditions of the black church in America; they just wanted some background music.

The Civil Rights Activist

You may be asking, "What is this category doing in a list of negative portrayals of black preachers?" I am not suggesting that preachers, black or white, who were or are involved with civil rights are not positive people. However, the suggestion made by movies and TV is that all a black preacher can hope to be is a civil-rights activist. The problem is that this is the only positive portrayal.

Unfortunately, this idea lends itself to the black preacher-politician myth. No longer is it acceptable for a black minister to concern himself with preaching and teaching the Bible. The only acceptable role for the black preacher is that of the preacher-politician whose chief concern in life is not the salvation of souls but the equal distribution of wealth and power among blacks and whites. Many people buy into this myth, being familiar with Dr. King's "I Have a Dream" speech, but they have never heard one of the many sermons he delivered as a pastor. In fact, many do not even know that King was ever a pastor.

For many people, any black preacher who does not fit into the mold of the preacher-politician has failed to fulfill his calling. The gospel is no longer enough. Salvation is no longer enough. Money, power, position, and equality—these are the new elements of the black preacher's gospel.

No, the civil rights activist is not a negative stereotype, but it is an inadequate one. It is inadequate because it denies the sufficiency and saving power of the gospel. It is inadequate in its emphasis on the rights of some and its deafening silence concerning the rights of others, such as the unborn. It is inadequate in its promotion of immoral and ungodly men who pass themselves off as spokesmen for the most high God, while many of them live like representatives of the kingdom of darkness. It is inadequate in its insistence on railing against the sin of racism while excusing other sins like adultery and homosexuality. Ultimately, this stereotype is woefully inadequate in its flat, one-dimensional portrayal of the black preacher as everything and anything but a preacher.

The News Media's Portrayal of Christians

The Angry White Man

Jerry Falwell is not the only conservative Christian that will answer calls from political television talk shows; it just seems that way sometimes. He is one of a small, handpicked number of "experts" that many shows are willing to bring on the air to discuss religious issues. Falwell is not chosen because of his political acumen or his moral and ethical insights, though he is lacking in neither. On the contrary, I believe Falwell is chosen because many people don't like him!

Please don't misunderstand what I am saying. I think Jerry Falwell is a brilliant, well-spoken, informed, and insightful man. I like him! The point I am making is that to the average American out there watching *Larry King Live*, he represents those fanatical fundamentalists whom they view as narrow-minded, arrogant, holier-than-thou, and completely out of touch. Therefore, it doesn't matter if he is right; people disagree with him because they don't like him.

Imagine the Presbyterian minister, Lloyd Olgivie, on a show about same-sex marriage. His public persona is that of a rational, levelheaded, even-tempered, and intelligent man. People might actually listen to what he has to say without pre-judging him as a radical fundamentalist. That is precisely why you won't see more of him on TV!

The Black Preacher/Politician

There are innumerable instances where either the Reverend Jesse Jackson or Al Sharpton have been paraded in front of television audiences as ad hoc representatives for the black community. Allow me to go on record: Jesse Jackson does not speak for me! Nor does he speak for many blacks who live and work on different levels of a stratified group of people and who are not some homogeneous unit being herded around by some self-appointed black preacher-politician leader.

There are many knowledgeable persons who claim that Jackson has embellished the closeness of his past association with Dr. King. In addition, recent revelation of a long-term affair with one of Jackson's young female assistants that resulted in the birth of an illegitimate child causes one to raise the question, "Why does the news media insist on thrusting this man before the public as the spiritual leader of black America?" Why not find a man whose commitment to the church is greater than his commitment to a political party? Why not find a man whose personal morality and behavior are less questionable? It's simple: such a man would explode the myth of the black preacher-politician and could actually lend credence to biblical Christianity.

The Academic Liberal

The classic example of the so-called academic-liberal point of view is the aforementioned Peter Jennings program, *The Search for the Historical Jesus.* Academic liberals comprised a major part of the endless coterie of talking heads brought out after the September 11 attacks who looked straight into the camera and told us all that Christians and Muslims worship the same God. It's always the same; you turn on the television and see a person whose name is completely unfamiliar speaking about an obscure biblical topic and offering opinions that no one with any real knowledge on the subject would agree with.

I am amazed when I turn on some PBS special or a History Channel documentary about Jesus or the Bible and hear from "scholars" at schools that I chose not to attend because of their antagonism toward orthodox Christianity. Where are the theologians from Dallas Theological Seminary or Trinity Evangelical Divinity School? Where are the professors from our conservative Southern Baptist seminaries? I'm not suggesting that these people should be the only experts consulted, but they should be consulted.

The Social Liberal

A couple of years ago, my home state of California voted on a proposition that would have given domestic partner benefits to gay couples. As I flipped though the channels one night, I caught a glimpse of one of the debates on the issue. I had seen several discussions, but this one was different. In one studio there was a gay Hollywood actor and the leader of the largest homosexual activist group in California who were both in favor of the proposition. In another studio there was a representative of a conservative homosexual group who opposed the proposition. In yet another location, there was Al Mohler, the president of the Southern Baptist Theological Seminary in Louisville, Kentucky. (Guess who was cast as the angry white man?) In yet another location sat a young woman who pastored a Methodist church in California. She was in favor of the proposition. It was like observing a train wreck. I couldn't turn away.

There were several instances that caused this show to be burned indelibly in my mind. One was when Al Mohler asked the two homosexual activists one of the most pointed, insightful, and revealing questions ever posed on the issue: What if a man wanted to marry his daughter; should we let him? The activists tried to shrug the question off as being ridiculous, but it wasn't.

The point was brilliant! Suppose their answer had been, "We can't let that happen, that is wrong." Then the next question would be, "Who are you to judge?" If the answer had been, "Let him do whatever he wants," then the next question would be, "Where does it end?" And perhaps a follow-up: "How can we then say that the child molester or the rapist is wrong when they do what 'feels right' to them?" These are powerful arguments! Unfortunately, Mohler was not allowed to carry his argument to its end. No TV reporter would have dared to allow it; to do so would have been intolerant.

Another moment that I will never forget was when the Methodist pastor chimed in and made known that she was in favor of same-sex marriage and domestic partner benefits. I asked myself, "Who is this woman, and why is she on the show?" The answer was obvious. She was there to demonstrate the fact that Mohler was merely an angry white man and not a true representative of the Christian perspective. She was there to prove that thoughtful, progressive Christians can get beyond the bias and bigotry of their holy books to see the big picture.

Is Balance Enough?

Some may say, "Sure, there are negative portrayals, but there are also some good ones." Let me respond in two ways. First, anyone paying attention would have to admit that the negative portrayals far outweigh the positive. In fact, the negative portrayals are so common that they have become cliché. One reason the stereotypes in this chapter are so easily recognizable is the frequency with which they appear. Trust me, few people who actually watch TV and movies will read this chapter and say, "The drunken lush? I wonder what he means by that?" We have all seen these portrayals, and they are far too common.

Second, speaking of balance in the portrayal seems rather ironic in light of the fact that other religious groups are treated with the utmost respect. Imagine a TV program with a drunken Buddhist monk or a lecherous rabbi (outside of the slapstick comedy genre). These would be shocking! In fact, one has to strain to remember the last time such a portrayal occurred. It is difficult to imagine the kind of stereotypical approaches used in the portrayal of Christian people being applied to members of other religious groups. And when they are, they represent the exception and not the rule. In order to understand the significance of this point, look at the media's treatment of a related issue, that of blacks and crime.

Recently, a well-known credit card company launched a series of commercials touting its security benefits. In each commercial, there is a woman whose purse is snatched, or about to be. After about the third one, I noticed something, the same thing I notice in virtually every commercial that depicts crime. The criminals, in this case the purse-snatchers, are rarely black. Why is this? Because marketers know that depicting blacks as criminals, except in TV dramas set in black settings and containing sufficient numbers of black protagonists to balance the show, is off-limits! They know that a commercial featuring a black purse-snatcher would set off an avalanche of phone calls, letters, and meetings with black leaders that would cost them far more than money.

How many times have we seen Jesse Jackson, Al Sharpton, and Louis Farrakhan parading before TV cameras while bemoaning the mistreatment of blacks in the media? In fact, these men's public personas are based on the fight against such racism. Jesse Jackson, for example, recently opposed the release of the film *Barbershop* because of its negative comments concerning Martin Luther King Jr. The comments highlighted Dr. King's penchant for infidelity, a charge few deny. Jackson didn't argue that King was a faithful husband but that highlighting such a fact sullies King's reputation and thus should not be allowed.

Another fascinating occurrence is the recent capture of the DC-area snipers. The adult suspect, John Muhammad, is a member of the Nation of Islam. In fact, there are claims that he served as a security officer for Louis Farrakhan during the Million Man March. What is so fascinating is that there has been virtually no mention of his Nation of Islam ties. Nor has there been any discussion of the tenets of the movement that could have fostered his animosity toward the United States. Why? When the 9/11 bombers were linked to Islam and eventually Al Qaeda there was an endless stream of Islamists explaining their actions in light of the Qur'an. Where are the Nation of Islam experts?

Let me reiterate; I am not asking TV to change. I do think that there is a time and a place to call the TV and movie industry to account, but that is not the goal here. The goal of this chapter is to shed light on the facts. Christians are portrayed negatively in the media. There is no denying that. Furthermore, changing this issue involves a lot more than just making people afraid to do it anymore. This is an issue that goes to the core of where we have arrived as a society. Religious relativism, tolerance, and philosophical pluralism leave no room for biblical Christianity. Therefore, the portrayal of Christians as narrow-minded buffoons is not an intentional slander; it is merely a reflection of perceived reality.

Many things in my heritage shape my attitude toward and response to this issue. For example, who among us has not been utterly mortified by the classic portrayals of black people in the cartoons of days gone by? We see the inordinately large lips, the bulging eyes, the pitch-black skin, and the apelike caricatures and we cringe—or at least, I hope you do. "How could anyone have drawn these?" we ask. I'll tell you how. They reflected what many people thought of the black race. To them this was an accurate though admittedly exaggerated portrayal. Aunt Jemima, for example, was not seen as an insulting caricature in those days. She was just "one of them."

When I look at these cartoons, my disdain for the images is matched only by the pride with which I view those who endured and eventually overcame that age. To the media they were high-functioning apes, but in their hearts they were a proud race of survivors. What strength, what courage, what endurance and determination! They were heroes.

I am not writing this book to beg the culture to treat us better. I am writing this book to encourage believers to stop expecting the culture to roll out the red carpet. This is not our home; we are just pilgrims passing through a barren land. We are the ones who have what the culture needs, so why should we be perceived as having our hands out? Besides, compliance without transformation is meaningless. Haven't we seen this in race relations? It is one thing for a company to hire a black man or woman because the government says it has to; it is quite a different story when the company hires the applicant because he or she is the most qualified applicant, with no regard to race.

4

"DON'T USE THAT NAME!"

Another reality of living in a post-Christian culture is the offensive nature of the name of Jesus. Countless names are immediately identifiable in our culture. Just say the names of Gandhi, Churchill, Hitler, Einstein, Jordan, Tiger, or Oprah, and people immediately recognize the person about whom you are speaking. The difference is that people in our culture are not threatened by the ideologies any of these people represent.

No one would forbid a high school or junior high student from writing a paper on Hitler, but let her write on Jesus and sparks will fly. A class valedictorian would be praised if he quoted Gandhi in a speech but punished if he quoted Jesus. A presidential candidate who considered Einstein as the greatest influence in his life would be considered highly intellectual, but when George W. Bush proclaimed Jesus Christ as the most influential person in his life, he set off a media firestorm! There is no room for the name of Jesus in a post-Christian culture.

The Sanhedrin didn't mind Peter and John being religious. They didn't even mind them preaching, teaching, and healing. They did, however, object to their doing these things in the name of Jesus. Thus, the Sanhedrin warned them to speak to no one in that name. Similarly, our culture has said to us, "Preach, teach, and practice Christianity all you want; however, when it comes to the public square, don't use that name!"

The Name of Jesus in the Public Square

While I was writing this chapter, I was preparing to preach in a citywide September 11 worship service in The Woodlands, Texas, a suburb of Houston. An ecumenical group in the area caught wind of the affair and invited themselves to join the sixteen area churches that were sponsoring the event. That is, until they learned that the service would include a biblical sermon.

The group went ballistic! They could not believe that Christian churches would get together for Christian worship on the anniversary of the terrorist attacks. They insisted that the event be ecumenical in nature and include addresses from a variety of religious leaders. In short, they did not want Jesus to be preached. Of course, the churches refused.

Eventually, the dispute went public. The press was notified and the event vilified. The story was carried on the local news and was eventually picked up by the Associated Press. One Jewish rabbi commented that the sponsors of this event were a bunch of fundamentalists and that there was no difference between them and the terrorists. Remarkably, many people agree with his point of view! The "tolerant" thing to do is to talk about God in general, nonoffensive terms. Putting Jesus into the public square is simply too divisive.

The Name of Jesus in the Public School

The name of Jesus is even more divisive in our public school systems. Let me be clear; while I do advocate students' rights to the free exercise of religion in schools, such as voluntary school prayers, I do not advocate open proselytization in public schools. Students represent a captive audience and should not be forced to listen to presentations designed to sway them toward one belief or another. Most of us are loathe to think of a radical Islamic group coming into our public schools to promote their ideas, but many have little problem with a Christian minister coming in and "preaching the gospel." Both possibilities are equally inappropriate. Who would decide which Christian groups are allowed? Who would handle the discipleship and follow-up?

I do, however, believe that it is impossible to educate children properly without addressing religion. How can one understand American history, for example, without understanding the influence of Christianity and the Bible? How can one explain the Renaissance without explaining the Reformation? And how can we explain the current crisis in the Middle East without explaining the foundational elements of Islam and Judaism that serve as the backdrop to current events? In short, education without religion is inadequate. Studying events and movements within their accompanying religious contexts, though, is a far cry from proselytizing students. Adding the religious background contributes to a balanced, thorough education. Tragically, such an approach was scrapped a generation ago.

Fortunately, the courts do allow student-led, student-initiated religious expression in school. Also, equal access laws assure the inclusion of religious groups in the overall fabric of a school's cultural atmosphere. For instance, it is illegal for the chess club and the Spanish club to be given a page in the yearbook while Christian groups are excluded. Christian legal advocacy organizations like the Rutherford Institute and the American Center for Law and Justice have made great strides in assuring the preservation of such rights.

Nevertheless, the fact remains. The name of Jesus is not welcome in many of our public schools. Consider these examples:

- Kandice Smith was an ordinary sixth grader in Walker County, Alabama, Bible Belt USA. Her parents gave her a necklace with a cross pendant, and she proudly wore it to school. To her surprise, she was instructed to remove the necklace because it violated school policy! Eventually, Kandice was allowed to wear her necklace, but not before pursuing her case all the way to U.S. District court.

- Another student in Orono, Maine, was asked to turn a T-shirt inside-out because it bore the name of Jesus Christ. The third-grader was told that her shirt was offensive to others and inappropriate for school.

- In December 2002, Fran Levy, principal of the Thomas Jefferson Magnet School of Humanities in Flushing, New York, acted in a way that illustrates discrimination against the name of Jesus. She issued a memo directing teachers to bring religious symbols to school for the holiday celebrations. Dr. Levy included Kwanzaa, Hanukkah, and an Islamic celebration but specifically excluded Christmas, according to the Rutherford Institute.

- A group of Christian students in Hampton, Virginia, hosted an Easter can drive to raise money for a women's shelter. Unfortunately, administrators at Kecoughton High School were displeased with the event, not because students were raising money for a shelter, but because they named it after a Christian holiday. The students were commanded to change the name of the event to Spring Can Drive.

The Name of Jesus at Christmas

"Happy Holidays!" That greeting wears me out! Why don't we say it on Memorial Day or Labor Day? Some argue, "We only say 'Happy Holidays' during November and December because there are so many holidays." Then why don't we say it at New Year's? That's right, New Year's Eve is closer to Christmas than Thanksgiving is, but as soon a Christmas is over, we stop saying "Happy Holidays." Isn't New Year's one of the holidays to which we refer when we use the phrase? Nevertheless, when the ball drops in Times Square, nobody yells, "Happy Holidays!" Even television newscasters seem to have no problem with shouting "Happy New Year!"

The phrase "Happy Holidays" has nothing to do with the number of holidays we celebrate during the season; it has everything to do with the offense of Christmas. Companies, schools, and government agencies are often not allowed to have Christmas parties. Television specials often refrain from using the word *Christmas* in their titles, and the phrase "Merry Christmas and Happy New Year" has been all but stricken from public discourse.

No one wants to come out and say it, but Christmas is politically incorrect. The Anti-Defamation League, for example, put out a set of guidelines for Christmas celebrations which addresses the placement of religious symbols such as crosses and nativity scenes. Concerning the erecting of them on public property, the ADL states the following: "[Their placement is] acceptable only if privately placed and disclaimer [sic] ensuring that viewers know that the government did not place or endorse the display."[1] In other words, a Christmas nativity scene can only be placed on public property if there is a notice to all viewers that the government had nothing to do with it. This restriction does not, however apply to a tree or other secular symbols. So Christmas is fine as long as it has no Christ.

In 1999, school board chairman John Douglas and the Newton County, Georgia, school board did the unthinkable. They changed the official school calendar to read "Christmas Holiday" instead of "Winter Holiday." The previous change had been made several years earlier due to pressure from proponents of political correctness. In September 2000, the ACLU contacted Mr. Douglas and insisted that the board change the calendar. They told Mr. Douglas that if the school board insisted on using the word *Christmas*, the ACLU would sue.

Imagine someone saying "If you use the word *Thanksgiving* on your calendar, we will sue you." Of course, proponents of political correctness will argue, "Calling a holiday Thanksgiving is not offensive to people of other religions." Perhaps not, but I suspect that some Native Americans might well be offended by the name of our November holiday. What about pacifists who are offended by the holiday called Veterans Day? There is always someone who may be offended.

The real argument, though, is not the possibility of offense, but the root of the word. That's right, the problem with Christmas is *Christ*. Hence the insistence on the use of the phrase Happy Holidays. What is interesting about this issue is the fact that the official name of the *federal* holiday is "Christmas." In other words, the Newton County School Board was warned not to use the name given to a holiday by the federal government in 1870!

No "God," Either!

Sometimes public offense goes beyond the name of Jesus to any reference at all to God. Patrick Cubbage, a Vietnam combat veteran, was an honor guard at the William C. Doyle Memorial Cemetery in North Hanover, New Jersey. He was fired for giving a blessing during funeral ceremonies that included the word *God*. In an Internet article on their official Web site, the Rutherford Institute, Cubbage's legal representative, gives this account:

> According to Cubbage, on those occasions when the deceased's family specifically requested a blessing, he would then proffer the following blessing, which is also customary according to the federal flag manual: "God bless you and this family, and God bless the United States of America." However, after a fellow honor guardsman complained about Cubbage's use of the blessing, his supervisor ordered him in mid-

October 2002 to stop referring to God. Cubbage immediately pointed to the section in the Flag Presentation Protocol pamphlet that said the blessing should be included as part of the graveside ceremony "if the next of kin has expressed a religious preference or belief." Nevertheless, Cubbage's supervisor insisted that he stop using the blessing because it might offend the families of veterans and other honor guardsmen. Cubbage reluctantly agreed to use the blessing only if the deceased veteran's next of kin specifically requested that it be included. On October 31, 2002, the son of a deceased veteran asked that Cubbage include the blessing in his graveside presentation. Shortly afterwards, a fellow honor guardsman reported the incident and Cubbage was fired for including the simple blessing in the graveside ceremony. As Cubbage remarked, "I just don't get it. When you give people that flag, you see them look into it and remember a whole time in their loved one's life. So why in God's name did they fire me? Because in God's name, they did fire me."[2]

At the time of publication, this case had yet to be decided.

Drawing a Line in the Sand

I am the worst kind of Texan—I am a Texan by choice. As we nonnatives say in the Lone Star State, "I wasn't born in Texas; I just got here as quick as I could." I don't think there is another state in America whose residents are as proud as those who wear the label "Texan." Consequently, I also don't know of another state whose residents catch more grief around the country. All kidding aside, though, Texans do have a rich and colorful history filled with legends and heroes that are larger-than-life.

Perhaps the biggest (not *largest* . . . this is Texas we're talking about) of these legends is the story of the Alamo. I will never forget the day my Texas history teacher told us about Jim Bowie, who was fully aware that the numerically superior forces of the Mexican Army were about to capture the fort. He drew a line in the sand and issued a challenge to his men, inviting all who were willing to stay and fight to the end to step across the line. Legend has it, every one of those men walked across that line in the sand. (Of course this part of the story was complete myth, but go along with me here).

Eventually, the battle was lost and the fort was overrun. Nearly all of those men died, but their courage and resolve served to inspire the remaining forces. "Remember the Alamo!" became the battle cry of Texas as her countrymen fought for and won their independence from Mexico.

While I am not suggesting that Christians take up arms in a literal way against our post-Christian culture, I am suggesting that it is time to draw our own line in the sand. We need to make a decision. Will we stay behind the line, letting the battle against religious relativism, tolerance, and pluralism overtake us, or will we step over it, standing up for the cause of Christ?

This section will examine three issues that cannot be overlooked if we are to choose the latter response. Chapter 5 is a challenge to engage the culture through the proclamation of the gospel. Chapter 6 explores the process of telling our story in a culture in which people believe that everyone's story is equal. Chapter 7 is an honest look at suffering for Christ, which is a real possibility for those who choose to cross this line drawn in the sand.

5

WE MUST PREACH

One of the most crucial questions for Christians in a post-Christian culture is this: Will we continue to preach? Practicing Christianity continues to cost us nothing. We can go to church, pray, read our Bibles, and even enjoy our holy days. However, preaching the gospel to those outside our ranks is crossing the line. Doing so opens us to the scrutiny and ridicule of society.

The apostles' response was bold and courageous. "Judge for yourselves whether it is right in God's sight to obey you rather than God. For we cannot help speaking about what we have seen and heard" (Acts 4:19–20). Their answer to the Sanhedrin is quite foreign to our ears. In a modern setting one would expect at least two alternative responses: (1) "Yeah, well, do you have any idea how many famous actors and athletes believe what we believe?" or (2) "You just wait until we get a few godly men on the Sanhedrin." I facetiously call these responses the "popular idol" and the "political savior" response.

The first problem with these responses is that they often serve as excuses for believers to wait for the work of proclaiming the gospel to be done by those whom we deem more qualified to do so. The second problem is that those individuals to whom we have given the responsibility of representing the Christian community in popular culture often fail to accomplish the task.

The popular idol is not enough.

"Hey, did you see so-and-so's performance in the World Series last year? I heard he is a Christian." I can't tell you how many times I have heard these statements and other similar comments about so-called Christian athletes. And how many times will I have to hear about half-naked singers and two-faced politicians who are "fine Christians?" On the outside I offer a polite, "You don't say?" However, I must admit that on the inside there is a raging, "Who cares?" dying to get out.

The issue isn't whether I care if athletes are going to heaven—or actors, politicians, and millionaire business owners for that matter. It's just that I care as much about my neighbor down the street getting there. Furthermore, when I watch a baseball player dropping profanities from the dugout at a rate that would make a sailor blush, or a performer singing about an illicit sexual liaison, the last thing I want to think about is the fact that he or she claims to be a follower of Christ.

The idea behind these conversations is simple. We live in a culture that worships superstars. This is nothing short of idolatry! The church in many instances has refused to rebuke this idolatry, choosing instead to embrace it. Now our goal is to bring the idols into the church, thus legitimizing our worship of them. Does this sound eerily familiar?

One church in the southern part of the United States recently spent $80,000 on an event that brought in a famous NFL star to "share the gospel." What made this event so unusual is that the church is a fledgling congregation that does not have enough money to purchase a building to meet in (not that you have to have that). Somehow they scrounged together almost three times the annual household income of an average family in the church to pay a millionaire to come talk to their community about Jesus.

And if that's not bad enough, after the event proved to be an utter failure, one of the church leaders said to me, "It didn't turn out the way we wanted, but I think the Lord may have just wanted us to minister to [the player], because he has a lot of growing to do." That's right! They spent $80,000 to bring in an athlete who is immature in the faith. He went on to say that he hoped the man's Jewish agent was touched. The entire conversation was disturbing but not surprising.

There is an unsettling trend in the thinking of many of today's church leaders. For some reason we have bought into the idea that the gospel needs help, or that those who proclaim the gospel need a platform. It is as though God is no longer enough.

I am not saying that a Christian's fame should prevent him or her from being heard. On the contrary, every Christian has an obligation to shout his or her faith from the rooftops. Nor do I mean to imply that people should not make a living preaching the gospel—they should. What I am saying is that the practice of paying for popularity in the church sends the wrong message. God is no respecter of persons; we shouldn't be, either.

Unfortunately, what ends up happening is a gross misrepresentation of the gospel. What's worse, these individuals often end up embarrassing the kingdom when the truth about their walk comes out. I don't have to name names; the media gleefully does that for me.

Another sad fact is that with few exceptions, the church throws these people away shortly after their brief moment at the top. Mike Singleterry, for example, was one of the most sought-after speakers in America when he was the cornerstone of the Chicago Bears' championship defense. The money he could command for sharing his testimony was astronomical. However, he has since retired from football and gone to seminary. Now he has actually been trained and has much more to say, but as popular speakers go, he has fallen off of the map.

I don't fault athletes and other celebrities for this trend, which is merely a symptom of a larger issue. Christianity has lost favor with our culture; instead of acknowledging that and accepting it, many believers have tried to prove that we are "cool" by pointing to the number of cultural icons who have cast their lot with us. Others have turned their eyes toward Washington in search of a political savior.

The political savior is not coming.

Another common crutch for Christians desiring mainstream acceptance is the man or woman who will change the political climate in America and restore the golden age of the 1950s. The expectation is that the right person at the helm could return this country to the days of *Leave It to Beaver*. Ironically, every time someone makes this comment and there are blacks in the audience, the blacks' wish always turns into "1950s without the racism." Unfortunately, one cannot separate the two. For those who would have been on the other side of the racial divide, there is no possible way to idealize the decade of the 1950s. Nevertheless, the quest remains the same. We want a political savior to transform our society. We expect a career politician to ride into Washington, DC, on a white horse, plop down his *New King James Study Bible*, and take apart every piece of legislation that does not agree with our interpretation of the Scriptures.

Allow me to be the first to say, no way! The problem with this wish is that it assumes several realities that are as close to impossible as one can get. First, it assumes that a person with that kind of prophetic edge could be elected to national office. Does the name Alan Keyes mean anything in this regard? And his being black has nothing to do with it. Colin Powell is black, and few people would be surprised if he followed George W. as the next president, or at least as the next Republican nominee. No, Alan Keyes's problem is not the color of his skin; it is the content of his rhetoric. He doesn't play the game. He, for example, would never debate the question of abortion without addressing the question of when life begins. He could care less about being characterized as a narrow ideologue.

The current furor over George Bush's use of religious language reinforces this point. When he ran for office, no one would have accused him of being an "Alan Keyes." However, the manner in which he has handled himself—his belief in good and evil, his use of the name of God, and his push for faith-based programs—has alienated a large segment of the population. It would not be surprising to see a tremendous backlash against any future candidate with strong religious convictions.

Second, this view assumes that such a candidate would be right in imposing his or her will on the nation. I find it interesting that when ideas come across the news wire with which we disagree, such as the recent Ninth Circuit Court decision that the words "under God" in the Pledge of Allegiance were unconstitutional, Christians cry foul. Why? Because we believe it is wrong for a three-person panel to dictate such things to the masses. I agree, but I must pose a question: What makes regulating our behavior any more appropriate when a "godly" president does it under the ideal of saving us from pagan immorality by imposing his will on us?

The truth of the matter is that we believe such a president would make it easier for us to live our lives. We would no longer be outcasts who had to go against the grain. We would no longer be referred to as narrow-minded bigots. We would no longer have to hold our tongues during discussions about moral issues on which we disagree with the government and society. In short, we would be relieved of our responsibility to be prophetic voices in a lost and dying world.

Don't forget that one of the most prophetic voices in recent history was not a politician. Who can forget Mother Teresa's speech at a 1994 prayer breakfast when she respectfully yet pointedly challenged a roomful of politicians on the issue of the sanctity of life? No one seeking votes would have spoken so boldly! The president and vice president, their wives, and a host of others, virtually all of whom held views contrary to those Mother Teresa espoused, sat quietly as she rebuked them.

The problem with the political savior is that he would have to be a politician and not a prophet.

The mandate to preach includes all of us.

Who can forget those moments as a child when a sibling or a friend looked us in the face and said, "Your mother said . . . ." Whatever followed was certain to elicit an immediate response. There is just something different about a command that comes from Mom. Unfortunately, God doesn't rate as high in many cases, probably because Mom can be a lot tougher at times (I love you, Mom). Seriously, the fact that God gives commands and sometimes withholds or delays his wrath often leads to delayed obedience, or worse yet, to disobedience. However, make no mistake: Whatever a man sows, he will also reap.

One area wherein God has spoken clearly and our response has been delayed is that of preaching the gospel to a lost world. Perhaps the most prominent example of this mandate is Jesus' Great Commission in Matthew 28:19-20: "Go therefore and make disciples of all the nations, baptizing them in the name of the Father and the Son and the Holy Spirit, teaching them to observe all that I commanded you; and lo, I am with you always, even to the end of the age." While there seems to be little room for debate as to what is being said in this passage, you might be surprised by the lengths to which some have gone to excuse themselves from its teaching.

"The Great Commission was for the apostles."

Some people argue that Jesus' command was only for those who heard it at the time. There are several problems with this position. First, if his commission was only for the apostles, then people throughout the world today were never meant to hear the gospel. This position is simply unacceptable. Scripture is clear that God intends for the gospel to be preached to *ta ethnē* (literally "every people group," v. 19). What is to be said of the Lord's promise in Acts 1:8? "You will receive power when the Holy Spirit comes on you; and you will be my witnesses in Jerusalem, and in all Judea and Samaria, and to the ends of the earth." Most of those who heard these words never even made it outside the Roman Empire.

A second problem is the context. If we accept the argument that the command "Go and make disciples" is not for us, then we must also concede that the promise "I am with you" is not for us, either. Thus arises a problem. Is Jesus not with those of us who follow him in the postapostolic age?

Finally, this argument ignores the clear implication of Jesus' command. He said, "teaching them to observe everything I commanded you." Guess what! This command means that the apostles were told to teach new disciples to reach the nations by teaching new disciples to reach the nations, by. . . . The point is clear. This phrase makes it virtually impossible to argue that the Great Commission was meant strictly for the apostles.

"This doesn't mean I have to preach; I can witness by my lifestyle."

There is definitely something to be said for the importance of lifestyle in evangelism. However, we have to keep it in its proper perspective. First, Jesus was clear. "Teaching them" in the passage's context comes from the Greek word *didaskē*, which means "to teach or speak." The instruction is to make audible proclamation of the gospel.

Second, my lifestyle is an insufficient example. Sometimes it sounds as though we expect our neighbors to say, "Look at the contentment and joy with which he mows his lawn or she pulls weeds in their flower beds. I must meet their God!" Something must be said! "How then will they call on Him in whom they have not believed? How will they believe in Him whom they have not heard? And how will they hear without a preacher?" (Romans 10:14).

"But I'm not a preacher!"

Neither were most of the apostles. One of the most amazing characters Jesus chose was Matthew (Levi). He was a tax collector, one of the most hated men of his day—or ours, for that matter. Granted, eventually he, like the rest of the apostles, became what we would refer to as a full-time minister of the gospel. However, before he became the author of what we know as the First Gospel, he was anything but a preacher.

God does not intend for the world to be won by preachers.

A lost and perishing world needs a word from God.

Ultimately, a believer's commitment to preaching the word must be born out of a passion for lost people. Until we realize that Jesus is the only way to salvation and that those who do not know him as Lord and Savior will perish, we will continue to trade obedience for security. However, once we get a glimpse of the reality and finality of the fate of the lost, we will preach Jesus.

My salvation experience and my passion for evangelism came almost simultaneously. I did not grow up going to church. In fact, during the formative years of my life, my mother experimented with several New Age religions until she finally settled on Buddhism. (Buddhism is not New Age, but it, along with Hinduism, forms the foundation for many New Age religions.) My father, whom she married after becoming pregnant as a seventeen-year-old high school senior, was not around. He and my mother had split up early in my childhood.

My mother was part of a growing group of young blacks in 1970s urban Los Angeles who were looking for something more, in a spiritual sense. She had seen the dark side of so-called Christianity when a member of our family who was a prominent leader in his church abused her and several other female members of our family. Further, she grew weary of the empty rituals that formed the basis of much of what she saw. She had enough of people who shouted and waved their hands on Sunday morning and cursed their children up one side and down the other by Sunday afternoon.

Ultimately, she went where she found people whose lives seemed to match their spiritual claims. She found a group of sincere people who loved and accepted her—and accepted me as well—as she was. She also found a group of people that lived disciplined spiritual lives. These people prayed and chanted for hours on end. Eventually, she fully accepted their way of life. My mom converted to Buddhism.

My mother never forced me to join her in her spiritual quest. I occasionally went to the gatherings she attended, and I occasionally joined her in her times of prayer and meditation. However, I never became a Buddhist. My spiritual journey would not take shape until much later in my life.

When I got old enough to experience the difficulty of growing up as a fatherless black boy in south central Los Angeles, my mother decided it was time for a change. Just as I was entering middle school, my mom and I pulled up stakes and went to live with my uncle, a retired Marine Corps drill instructor, in Beaufort, South Carolina. It was like living with G.I. Joe! Trust me; I got out of trouble in a hurry. It was the most incredible thing I had ever experienced. Not only did I have a man in my life for the first time, but this guy had done three (count 'em: one, two, three) tours of duty in Vietnam; he was a bona fide hero! It was one of the greatest things that ever happened to me.

Eventually, not wanting me to return to Los Angeles, my mother moved us to San Antonio, Texas. During my senior year in high school, I experienced a painful personal loss that opened my eyes to the question of eternity. My cousin, Jarmal Walker, was just a few months younger than I. He was the closest thing to a brother that I ever had. The two of us were inseparable, or so we thought, though he had not left the mean streets of L.A. In fact, he had gotten caught up in "the life." He had become a drug dealer. One day, during a drug deal in Oakland, someone walked up to Jarmal and shot him in the head. He was sixteen years old, and he was dead.

Despite the objections of many, I returned to Los Angeles and attended Jarmal's funeral. I will never forget the day I walked past his casket and looked inside. He was only a few months younger than I, and he was gone. It was the saddest moment I had ever experienced. At times I was so distraught that I simply could not cry. I will never forget the look on his father's face. I never want to see anything like that again.

Eventually, I went off to college. It was there that my life would change forever. My father is about six feet five inches tall, and in his prime he weighed about 250 pounds. He played college football at Redlands University and eventually played professionally until injury prematurely ended his career. While he didn't give me much of the paternal influence I needed, he gave me some great genes! I was recruited by over one hundred colleges and universities, some to play football, some to run track (decathlon), and others for academics (thanks, Mom!). I chose football.

My freshman year was a landmark one. It was that year that I heard the gospel for the very first time. Steve Morgan, with Campus Crusade, came into the locker room one day to talk to me about FCA (the Fellowship of Christian Athletes). He saw in my bio that I had been involved in the organization in high school. What he didn't know was that my high school coach had basically come out of his office one day and said, "Men, we are going to have FCA! Take these shirts and wear them on Tuesday!" That was it. He had occasionally told us to get into groups and discuss things like staying drug free, but there had been nothing more to it.

It took Steve about five minutes to realize that I did not know Jesus from the man in the moon. He started an evangelism presentation using the Evangelism Explosion approach, but as with other similar presentations, it was based on several foundational premises that did not apply to me—the existence of God, the Bible, the historicity of Jesus, and other issues. I simply did not yet share many of the assumptions necessary to follow the presentation.

So, eventually, Steve stopped his presentation and backed up. He held up his Bible and said, "This is a Bible." He began to explain how God had revealed himself in the Bible and how the Bible was unlike any other holy book. He walked me through the message of the Bible step-by-step. He explained the fall of humanity and its implications. He explained the redemption God provided and offered in Jesus. Eventually, he went back to his presentation and walked me through the gospel. We would meet every day. He would explain more of the gospel. I would ask questions, and he would answer them or tell me to hold on until he could find an answer, and we would continue. In all, the process took about three weeks.

At last, I got it! The picture became clear. I, like every other human being, was a sinner. I owed a debt to God that I could not repay. I had to be redeemed, or I would experience separation from God for eternity because God and sin cannot cohabit. Christ had died for my sin, satisfying the righteous requirement of the Father. By faith, Christ's death could atone for my sin as I trusted him to substitute his righteousness for my sinfulness. I got it! The only problem was that Steve hadn't arrived yet that day to meet with me. I didn't know what to do, so I got down and lay prostrate on the floor. I said to God, "God, that thing that you did for Steve that he has been telling me you want to do for me . . . Now's good."

The greatest thing Steve ever did for me was not to ask me to change my prayer. He knew what I had gone through. He saw the lights come on. He knew that I didn't have, nor did I need, "church" words. He also knew that I was sincere and that I trusted Christ alone for my salvation.

When he entered the room, I was still on the floor weeping. When he looked into my eyes, he realized that I wasn't crying tears of joy that flowed as a result of the saving grace of God being manifested in my life. I looked at him and simply said, "I should be able to pick up the phone right now and call Jarmal." All I wanted to do was tell my cousin about Jesus. I wanted to tell him about the God who had just changed my life, but I couldn't. He had died six months earlier, and I would never get the chance to share this life-changing experience with him.

I have no idea what happened in Jarmal's spiritual life. We would all like to believe that our loved ones who have died have gone on to "a better place," but the truth may be quite different. I hope I see Jarmal again some day, but I doubt that I will. The only way I could have known that he heard the gospel is if I had shared it with him. I tremble as I write these words, knowing that members of my family are going to read this book and probably won't like the fact that I raise this issue. Moreover, most readers of this book will have also lost someone about whom they are not sure. Our normal response is to try to justify their salvation by some means. However, if their experience does not include the biblical realities that Steve had summarized for me and that believers know to be true, we cannot make such assumptions.

I faced a devastating reality. I could not bear to think that he was gone and I would never be able to share the good news of

Jesus with him. Then it happened! Steve looked at me and said, "There's nothing we can do about Jarmal, but is there someone else you can call?" You bet there was! I called my mother and later my father, both of whom are now on their way to glory! I called other relatives and friends and told everyone I could think of about what had happened to me. In all, the Lord gave me the privilege of leading about two dozen people to faith in Christ that semester.

God used Jarmal's death to ignite a flame in me. I don't believe God caused Jarmal's death, but I know he used it. I know I still think of him, and there are days I still ask why. But I trust God. I know that he is sovereign and that everything that comes into my life has been sifted through his hand. So I press on, fueled by a desire never again to feel the dread of missed opportunity.

The battle rages in the marketplace of ideas.

The book of Jude is one of the shortest and most power-packed letters in the New Testament. Jude wastes neither time nor words in his exhortation to the saints. The crux of his letter is found in the first few verses, where we learn that there is a battle being waged in the marketplace of ideas (my terminology, not Jude's).

First, this battle includes every believer. Jude addresses his comments to "those who have been called, who are loved by God the Father and kept by Jesus Christ." In other words, calling all Christians! Make no mistake about it; if you name the name of Jesus as your Lord and Savior, if you have been born again, and if you've been washed in the blood of the Lamb, you have been included in this clarion call.

Second, this battle is an essential element of the Christian's responsibility. One of the most poignant statements in the entire letter is this statement in verse 3: "Dear friends, although I was very eager to write to you about the salvation we share,

I felt I had to write and urge you to contend for the faith that was once for all entrusted to the saints." Did you catch that? He intended to write about salvation, but the Holy Spirit (under whose inspiration the Bible was written) evidently had other plans. Imagine the president of the United States writing his State of the Union address but changing his subject at the last minute. That would be news!

Third, this battle has infiltrated our ranks. Jude says: "Certain men . . . have secretly slipped in." Here he alludes to the fact that the battle in the marketplace of ideas is not just a battle with those who openly oppose Christianity, or are simply deceived, but with those on the inside as well. Jude indicates that these individuals represent more than just harmless dissent. They are malevolent, as indicated by Jude's classification of them as those "whose condemnation was written about long ago."

Fourth, failure to engage in this battle will have at least two colossal consequences. One consequence is that they will "change the grace of our God into a license for immorality." The other consequence is that they will "deny Jesus Christ our only Sovereign and Lord" (v. 4). His words could have been written yesterday! Jude could easily have been referring to those who push for a new homosexual theology, or to the proponents of the Jesus Seminar's aberrant Christology. This type of teaching, according to Jude, must be countered by the truth; the faith that was "once for all entrusted to the saints."

I recently preached at an evangelism conference where my message was preceded by the testimony of a forty-eight-year-old dentist who had come to faith just three years earlier. Interestingly, he had gone to church as a child and was a member of a church for years before he came to Christ. The problem was that he was the member of a church that in his words "never preached the gospel" and "never wanted to offend anyone." His church was characterized by the licentiousness and denial of

Christ described in Jude. As a consequence, he thought he was fine with God—because he was a member of a church—when, in fact, he was not. Tears filled his eyes when he spoke of the radio preacher who had shared a clear, concise presentation of the message of salvation that brought him out of darkness and into the marvelous light. He was also very emotional when he recalled the years he spent with those who had, in the words of Jude, "secretly slipped in."

Unfortunately, the dentist's experience is not an isolated one. There are people all around us who have fallen prey to falsehood within the church. Misrepresentation is rampant, and truth seems to be in short supply. There is only one answer as we face this epic battle in the marketplace of ideas: we must preach!

6
EVIDENCE THAT
CANNOT BE DENIED

One of my favorite pastimes is cooking for my family. In fact, I am so taken with cooking that my wife and children have begun to buy me cooking utensils for birthdays and Father's Day. There's just one problem. My son has severe food allergies. There are a couple of ways we deal with this. Either I cook meals that don't include the foods to which he is allergic, or I prepare a substitute for the offending items when I fix his plate.

One day, while we were living in England, I got my hands on some fresh Scottish salmon. I couldn't wait to grill it. My wife gently reminded me that our son is allergic to fish and that I should make him something else. I quickly reminded her that he had only had allergic reactions to catfish and trout. The only way we would know if he is allergic to salmon is for him to try it. Besides, I thought I remembered his eating salmon before.

We started with a creamy tomato soup that we had discovered at a local store—boy, do we miss that soup now that we're back in the States! Then came the salad; everything was going fine. Finally came the main course. My wife looked at me with that look—the one women get when we men are about to do something stupid, but they have already warned us and know that we have to learn the hard way. I laid the plates on the table, and we began to eat.

My son took a bite of his rice and immediately stopped eating. We all looked at him helplessly as he said those four words with which we are all too familiar, "My lips are itching!" He hadn't even touched the salmon; some of the juice had merely mingled with his rice. We immediately ran for his allergy medicine, but within minutes his lips had swelled to about twice their normal size. My wife looked at me again and shook her head. I felt terrible!

Later we all laughed about the episode—even my son. It was a typical moment in which Dad didn't listen to Mom and the results were horrific. My wife even took pictures to remind me of what my stubbornness had done to our son. As everything returned to normal, and my wife, rocking our eight-year-old son in her lap, asked me, "Will you listen to me next time?" I bowed my head in shame and said the only thing a dad could say at a moment like that . . . absolutely nothing!

I was speechless because the evidence of my error was staring me in the face. What could I say? Had my son never tried the salmon, my wife and I could have continued to argue about whether my son was allergic to it. However, that question has been settled because we have all seen the evidence.

The same can be said of a culture that denies the truth of God's word.

The members of the Sanhedrin realized that there was a man running around town who once was lame. They had likely walked by the man themselves on several occasions. Some may even have given him alms before. Now he was healed. What could they do? They had to threaten Peter and John and hope for the best. We can almost read their thoughts: *Hopefully, this healing is temporary. Hopefully, the attention will wane. Hopefully, this won't happen again. Hopefully, people won't make the connection between what happened to this man and the apostle's proclamation of Jesus.*

Ultimately, all they could do was hope. Why? Because it is impossible to argue with evidence when it is staring you in the face. Whether our culture agrees with our worldview, it cannot deny the evidence of our testimony. However, there are some ground rules that apply. Not every testimony is an effective testimony.

Everyone has a testimony and not all of them testify to the truth.

One of my favorite testimonies of transformation is that of a young man who was born in Omaha, Nebraska, in 1925. He grew up in rural Michigan in the 1930s and 1940s. He was a poor black boy whose father was a Baptist preacher. One day his father was killed in a racial incident. Eventually, the boy and his siblings were forced to go into foster care because his mother could no longer care for them.

He was a bright boy, but was never given a chance to pursue his dreams. When he spoke to his teachers about his career goal of becoming a lawyer, he was often told, "That's not a realistic goal for a colored boy." He began to lose interest in school and ultimately dropped out.

He went to Boston to live with his oldest sister. There he began a life of crime. Ultimately, he ended up in prison in 1945. There he met a man who told him of a way he could turn his life around. This man preached to him regularly. In time, he began to listen. One night in 1947, while in his cell, he says the Messiah came to visit him. His life was changed from that moment on. He became a model prisoner and a devout believer.

Upon his release from prison in 1952, he poured himself into his faith. He became a preacher of national renown. His name became a household word. He was no longer a drug addict and a criminal. He had been completely changed. He single-handedly planted over one hundred houses of worship and influenced an entire generation.

His name? Malcolm X. That's right, the militant Nation of Islam leader who was eventually converted to orthodox Islam and who was later assassinated by members of the group to which he once belonged. "The Messiah" to whom he referred was Elijah Muhammad, the leader of the Nation of Islam. Eventually, Malcolm X recognized the Nation of Islam as a cult. Nevertheless, his life was changed.

There are several things we learn from the life of Malcolm X. First, *experiences can be misleading*. He saw and heard what he claimed was the Messiah. He had a vision in his cell and later met the man whom he said he had encountered. I don't know what produced Malcolm's experience. I believe it was a demonic force. Nevertheless, his experience, real though it may have been, was ultimately misleading, by his own admission.

Second, *a changed life is not irrefutable evidence*. Malcolm X was a new man. He got off drugs; he stopped womanizing; he quit gambling; he stopped stealing; he was changed! Nonetheless, what he believed turned out to be a lie. There are many people today whose lives have been changed by what they perceive to be truth. However, in many instances, their "truth" turns out to be no more than self-delusion.

If this is true, then how can we know anything? How can we know that our experience is both real and true? How can we know that our faith is founded upon the rock and not merely upon sinking sand? How can we know that our God is God?

Our experience must be founded in truth.

Malcolm X's story illustrates that experience in and of itself is not enough. The man he thought was the Messiah was a womanizing, money-hungry cult leader whose teachings were anything but true. Malcolm learned that experience, even experiences that change lives, could be wrong. Our experience must be founded upon truth.

Many people who participate in trials for new drugs are given placebos. Often they think they are getting the real drug when all they have been taking is a sugar pill. Nevertheless, many of them claim to feel much better, and they praise the new drug's effectiveness. Their experience is a prime example of one that is not founded in truth.

Just because a person's life is better does not mean that his god is real. There are Mormons, Jews, Catholics, Buddhists, evangelicals, and pagans who claim to have had religious experiences that changed their lives. Everyone has a testimony! However, as stated earlier in our discussion of religious relativism, we can't all be right. Some experiences are grounded in truth, while others are merely placebos. Ultimately, there must be a standard. I believe that standard is the Word of God, the Bible.

The apostle Peter addresses his second epistle to "those who have received a faith of the same kind as ours, by the righteousness of our God and Savior, Jesus Christ" (2 Peter 1:1). The fact that this letter was a strong response to false teaching and persecution makes clear that Peter was making a clear distinction between those who claim to have met Christ and those who actually know him. In fact, Peter uses some form of the word *know* no fewer than nine times in the first chapter of his letter.

The source of this knowledge, according to Peter, is the Bible. He says of God's revelation, "His divine power has given us everything pertaining to life and godliness, through the true knowledge of Him who called us by His own glory and excellence" (v. 3). While some may argue that this knowledge is some sort of mystical insight, the context of the chapter does not allow for such an interpretation. One of the next statements asserts that "by these He has granted to us His precious and magnificent promises." To what could the "precious promises" refer if not to the Scriptures? The context of his argument is seen more clearly toward the end of the chapter when he states, "For know this first of all, that no prophecy of Scripture is a matter of own's own interpretation" (v. 20).

Many Christians claim to have had experiences where God "told" them something or did something in their lives that is inconsistent with Scripture. I have had two men tell me that God told them to divorce their wives. In both instances the reasons had nothing to do with Scripture. One man claimed he simply fell in love with another woman who was a better Christian than his wife. His argument was that God did not want him to be miserable. I asked him if he realized how much of the Bible would have to be rewritten for God to tell him such a thing.

On another occasion a gentleman became angry with me because of my response to his prayer request. He was engaged to a nonbeliever, and they were having problems. He asked me to pray that God would smooth things out. My response was a resounding "No!" Why on earth would I ask God to fix a problem that exists in part because of direct disobedience to his Word? The Bible is clear: "Do not be bound together with unbelievers" (2 Corinthians 6:14). We can't ask God to bless our disobedience and expect him to smile on that.

The gentleman's response was that he had prayed about it and that God had "given him a peace." What on earth does that mean? How can we say, objectively, that God was the one who gave that sense of peace? In order for that to be the case, at least two things would have to happen. First, God would have to be in the business of overriding the Scriptures. Second, there would have to be some objective criteria by which we could judge God's override, and that criteria would have to come from Scripture. In other words, it can't happen. I cannot objectively claim to have received a sense of peace from God about something that directly contradicts his Word.

Imagine the chaos that would accompany such a practice. One person says, "I have a peace about worshipping other gods." Another person says, "I have a peace about marrying three women." Where would it end? This reasoning is similar to the problem of philosophical pluralism discussed earlier. Philosophical pluralism claims that there is no truth, whereas this type of subjectivism claims that truth is contingent upon the individual. At the end of the day, the result is the same.

Imagine that you wake up one morning to the sound of hammering, sawing, and clanking wood. You walk outside and find that your neighbor has removed your fence and placed it fifty feet closer into your yard. When you ask him why he did it, he replies, "I woke up this morning, looked at the fence, and realized that I did not have enough room to add a pool, so I decided to move your fence over a bit." You begin to explain to him the false reasoning behind his actions and the fact that he can't just take your property, to which he replies, "I know my deed doesn't entitle me to this land, but when I thought it over, I got a peace about taking it."

This conversation may sound ridiculous, but the principle is the same. We do not change what is established because we feel like we have special permission. If this is true with laws established by men, how much more so with the law of God? Before we go telling people what God said or did in our lives, we have to make sure that what we are saying is founded on Scripture. The Bible is our final authority in all matters (2 Timothy 3:16; 2 Peter 1:3; Hebrews 1:1–2). Even the apostle Paul, when defending the truth of the resurrection against those who argued that there would be none, did not go directly to his experience; he started with Scripture (1 Corinthians 15).

Our experience must be corroborated.

The marketplace of ideas is like a court of law. We would never think of going to court with uncorroborated evidence.

Imagine trying to defend yourself against an allegation and the only thing you can say is, "I know I didn't do it." Or imagine trying to prove a case without documents, witnesses, or evidence to show the jury. The sad fact is that in many cases, this is all our culture requires. Religious relativism and philosophical pluralism have created an environment where all a person needs is an experience. Imagine, then, how much more powerful our testimony will be when it is corroborated.

In a world where all truth is measured by experience, corroboration is key. It is important that we let the world know that, unlike so many others, our experience does not exist in a vacuum. Our experience is both founded in Scripture and corroborated by the experiences of others throughout history. That's what's so great about the Bible!

The Bible was written on three different continents: Europe, Asia, and Africa. It was also written in three different languages: Hebrew, Aramaic, and Greek. Moreover, it was written by over forty authors from many different walks of life: shepherds, fishermen, generals, preachers, and tax collectors. And it was written over a period of fifteen hundred years (more about this later). Nevertheless, there is complete corroboration of the Bible's story line. Compare that to the Qur'an, for example, which is presented as the work of one man with absolutely no corroboration.

In 1 Corinthians 15, Paul corroborates his story by pointing to the others who saw the resurrected Christ: Peter, the Twelve, and a crowd of more than five hundred people at one time. In the first chapter of Galatians, he refers to the validation of his apostleship by Peter and James (v. 18). In both cases it was not enough that he had an experience; his experience had to be corroborated. So how do we corroborate our testimony? I'm glad you asked!

Subject your experience to the Scripture test.

The Bible is the final, ultimate authority for all matters of faith and practice. Therefore, the best question you can ask yourself when you have a questionable experience is, "What does the Bible say about this?" The Scripture clearly teaches that God has already given us everything we need for life and godliness in the Bible (2 Peter 1:3). If that is the case, then anything that comes to me from God is going to have to line up with what he has already revealed in the Bible.

Subject your experience to the body test.

One of the greatest gifts God has given us is the body of Christ, the church. Christianity is not lived in a vacuum. We belong to the Lord and to one another. The church is filled with men and women who have been walking with the Lord for years—in some cases, even decades. We must take advantage of these incredible resources.

Oftentimes when people have experiences that run counter to the views of the body of believers, they simply find another place to fellowship. For instance, many homosexuals who consider themselves Christians simply assume that their experience is right and that the majority of Christians are wrong, so they search out a church that will accept their point of view.

Granted, there are times when a body of believers is wrong about an issue. Take, for instance, the issue of segregation. Many churches continue to give tacit approval to the idea that blacks should only worship with blacks and whites should only worship with whites. In such cases Scripture always overrides the opinion of the body. We must consider both Scripture and the body of believers when testing the validity of our own experience.

Subject your experience to the worldview test.

Finally, we must ask, "Does this experience fit within the confines of a Christian worldview?" If I am a follower of Christ and I win the lottery, I cannot automatically jump to the conclusion that God approves of gambling. I choose this example because I have heard it more than once. The argument goes something like this: "God is in control of everything, so if he did not want me to gamble, he would not have allowed me to win." The same logic could be applied to any list of vices. One could say, for example, "God is in control of everything, so if he wanted me to be faithful to my husband, he would not have allowed me to meet and fall in love with another man"— another argument I have heard.

Aside from the fact that each of these issues fails the Scripture test, they also fail the worldview test. Such an approach to life would be virtually unlivable. Following this logic all the way through would lead to a worldview that says, "Whatever happens, whether good or bad, moral or immoral, must be God's will." Also, one would have the added difficulty of explaining all those times he or she did not hit the jackpot or find the "other" man or woman.

When used in concert, these three tests will keep the believer on track as it relates to personal experience. If we take each experience and sift it through these three filters, we will find ourselves exercising true biblical discernment, and we will be a great deal less likely to commit our culture's foremost error of allowing experience to be the foundation upon which we build our case for truth.

Our experience must be communicated effectively.

First Corinthians 15 is a tremendous example of a simple, concise, and effective method of communicating our experience to a culture short on truth. The process consists of three simple steps. First, refer to the biblical support for your claim (vv. 3–4). Next, corroborate your claim by placing it into the context of the historical experiences of other believers (vv. 5–7). Finally, tell your own story (vv. 8–11).

If I want to testify about my salvation experience, first I refer to biblical support for my claim. The Bible says that we are sinners (Romans 3:23) and that our sin separates us from God (Isaiah 59:2). The Bible also states that God provided forgiveness for us in Jesus (Romans 5:8; 6:23; 1 Peter 3:18, among other passages). Next, I corroborate these facts: I met several people who had come to this realization and had been born again. Finally, I tell my own story: Eventually, I trusted Christ and my life was transformed.

We can employ the same pattern for any biblical experience. As I said, this structure is not the only way to testify. It is, however, a tool that you can use to remind you to base your testimony on the truths found in Scripture and corroborated by the church throughout history. This validation of Scriptural truth sets Christianity apart from all other religions.

We must learn the art of testimony.

There is a neat story tucked away in the fourth chapter of the Gospel of John. It tells of the encounter between Jesus and the woman at the well, which is incredible in itself; but in a larger sense, it is the story of the woman at the well and the rest of Samaria. After coming to faith in Jesus, the woman at the well testifies of her encounter with Christ. As a result of her story, the entire region is impacted.

The beauty of this woman's testimony is its simplicity: "Many of the Samaritans from that town believed in him because of the woman's testimony, 'He told me all things that I have ever done'" (John 4:39). While her statement may not be every word she said to them, it is a synopsis of her testimony. There are several aspects of her story that we should apply to our efforts to testify.

Be brief.

There is a difference between a testimony and a life story. How many times have we heard people give their testimony beginning with the familiar disclaimer, "They told me I had ten minutes and there is no way I can share my testimony in that time, but I'll try." That is a person who does not know the difference between a testimony and a life story. A testimony is a brief explanation of how and when we met Jesus and what he has done in us since then. Ten minutes is more than enough time for that. In fact, if you are planning to share your testimony with strangers, you had better learn how to do it in three minutes!

Most people have little patience for testimonies about Jesus. They don't mind talking about religion and spirituality, but put Jesus in the mix and alarms go off. The beauty of this woman's testimony is due in large part to its brevity. She said so much with so few words.

Be humble.

How many times have you heard a testimony that did more to increase your esteem of the one who testified than it did to enhance your regard for Christ? Some people spend more time recounting their personal accolades than they do extolling the virtues of their Savior. This is not the case with the woman at the well. She brings virtually no attention to herself.

I am not saying that we should avoid telling people the truth about where we come from. A guy who sold his business in order to follow the Lord should say so. There is, however, a way to say it. The key is humility. Remember, it is not possible to make much of Jesus and make much of yourself at the same time.

Be honest.

The subtle candor of the woman at the well's testimony is fascinating! It is likely that everyone knew her story. She could easily have tried to make herself sound less guilty, less tainted. She could have made excuses for the direction her life had taken, but she didn't. She could have deflected the blame, but she didn't. She simply stated the facts: "He told me all the things I have done."

Another tact people take is to exaggerate their sin. We get in front of people and decide that the magnitude of the sin from which we were saved was insufficient so we embellish. All of a sudden a guy who had one scuffle on the playground in the fourth grade becomes a rough dude who "fought all his life." Or a man who had too much to drink one night at a fraternity party suddenly becomes a guy who was "delivered from a terrible addiction." In both instances the statements are dishonest! God does not gain more honor when we make ourselves sound worse than we actually were.

Be discreet.

There is a fine line between honest transparency and indiscretion. I bought a CD once with a collection of gospel songs. When it arrived, we put it in our CD player and began to enjoy this incredible collection of songs and singers. It was a real blessing—that is, until we listened to one of the tracks that contained a testimony (actually more of a life story) by one of the artists.

It had been recorded during the live concert. About five minutes into her story, we had to skip the track. Our two children, who were very young, were sitting in the back seat, and for the first time we had to protect them from the content on a Christian CD. This woman was so graphic in her description of the events of her life that it made us uncomfortable. Was it true? Yes! But just because something is true doesn't mean it needs to be said publicly without discretion.

The woman at the well doesn't recount the horrible details of her sin. She doesn't talk about the times, dates, and details of her liaisons. She doesn't use graphic or explicit language. Listen to the discretion in her statement: "He told me all the things I have done." Even though everyone who knew her would have known the details of her sin, anyone who was unaware of the details would also clearly have gotten the point.

Another key to her discretion is that she doesn't testify for anyone else. She doesn't say, "He told me that what Bob and I did wrong." If Bob wants to testify, he can speak for himself. I have actually heard men testify about the massive amounts of alcohol they used to drink and the number of women they chased, pointing to other men in the audience who did it with them. First of all, anyone who knows these men knows who they ran with. Second, they had no right to testify for others. What if the other people they mention haven't dealt with those things yet? What if they haven't come clean with their friends and family yet?

Be eager.

"The pastor stopped me on the way in this morning and asked me if I would share a testimony." If I am the guest preacher at this service, this is the point when my stomach starts to do cartwheels. But it could be worse; this statement could be followed by another worse one: "Pray for me. I really don't know what to say." At this point that guy who lives inside my head (who is not quite as "godly" as I am) wants to stand up and shout, "Then shut up and sit down!" I know, however, that my loud command probably wouldn't be the proper one for a preacher to yell in church. But I must admit that I cannot help but imagine lost people in the audience thinking, *I guess his God hasn't done anything for him lately.*

There ought to be an eagerness about us when we have the opportunity to share what God has done in our lives. I know that some people fear public speaking; that's not what I'm talking about. There is a difference between trepidation about speaking and having nothing to say. The woman at the well serves as a model in that she was eager to share. By the way, if you are afraid to speak in front of people, the worst thing you can do is say, "I'm really nervous." That will likely make it worse.

Be sensitive.

One of the greatest mistakes we make in our testimonies is to make the extreme sound normal. For instance, a multimillionaire businessman says, "We just put the Lord first in our business, and he did the rest." Or a former drug addict who says, "I prayed to receive Jesus, and the next moment I lost my craving for drugs. If you are struggling with addiction, just turn it over." Or a Super Bowl MVP who says, "I just prayed hard and followed the Lord and he blessed me, and if you just pray hard and follow the Lord, he will bless you, too." Or someone else who tells us, "Remember, we can do all things through Christ who strengthens us." All of these statements may be true, but what we don't realize is that sometimes the way we say them communicates more than we intend.

That millionaire businessman's words, for example, could imply that other businessmen in the room are just not honoring God enough in their business, and if they did, their success would be guaranteed. The Super Bowl MVP can almost come across the same way. And the delivered drug addict, if he is not careful, can seem like he or she is suggesting that anyone who struggles to defeat an addiction is not as "saved" as he or she is. Could it be that the businessman is just more adept at doing what he does than his competitors? Could Miss America just have been more beautiful and more talented? Could the Super Bowl MVP have just been bigger, stronger, faster, and worked harder than anyone else in the NFL? Of course! That's why there are far more lost people who have held these honors than there are Christians.

In some ways I am glad that Bill Gates, Michael Jordan, and Tiger Woods do not claim to follow Christ. If they did, people would be using them to prove that if you follow the Lord, he can make you number one! Well, they don't follow the Lord as far as we know, and they are arguably the best in the history of the known universe at what they do. There are Christian businessmen who walk with God and fail in their business; there are Christian men and women who struggle for years to overcome their addictions; and most of the best players in professional sports don't walk with God.

This is important to recognize because there are people all over this land who are made to feel like they are just not godly enough because of these insensitive approaches to testimony. They need to hear the millionaire businessman say, "I'm no more godly than anyone else, but for some reason he has put me in the right place at the right time, and if I lose it all tomorrow, he is still good."

I became painfully aware of this testimonial insensitivity one Sunday morning as I stood at the back door of a small church shaking hands with the congregation as they left (yes, there are places where they still do that). The pastor stood next to me and introduced me to several of the members. As one man passed by, he said, "This is Bill (not his real name); God has really blessed his business." As it turns out, Bill was the wealthiest man in town. I shook Bill's hand and exchanged pleasantries, then turned to meet the next man in line. "This is Joe (not his real name)," the pastor said. Joe shook my hand and said sarcastically, "I'm not as blessed as Bill."

At that moment it dawned on me. What the pastor had just done is equate blessings with money and relegate everyone else in that line to second-class status, not only in the community but also in the kingdom of God! Why didn't he say that God had really blessed Joe's business? Because Joe doesn't make a fraction of the money Bill does. I wonder what the pastor would say if Bill's business was ravaged by the current state of the stock market. Would he say, "This is Bill. God has really cursed his business." I don't think so. We need to be careful about what we communicate when we testify.

Final Thoughts

In an age where everyone is looking for an experience to justify what they choose to believe, those of us who follow Christ must avoid the temptation to lean on our experience as our only source of evidence. What separates the follower of Christ from adherents of other faiths is the fact that our experience is based in the person of the incarnate Son of God.

7

THE JOY OF SHARING IN HIS SUFFERING

After experiencing the onset of persecution, Peter and John returned to the other believers, not for a "pity party" but for a spontaneous prayer and praise meeting (Acts 4:23–31). Their response was not one of apprehension or fear, but of faith. They reminded God of what he did when Jesus was opposed and eventually killed. They prayed:

Indeed Herod and Pontius Pilate met together
with the Gentiles and the people of Israel in this city
to conspire against your holy servant Jesus, whom you
anointed. They did what your power and will had
decided beforehand should happen. Now, Lord, consider their threats and enable your servants to speak
your word with great boldness. Stretch out your hand
to heal and perform miraculous signs and wonders
through the name of your holy servant Jesus (Acts
4:27–30 NIV).

The key to their faith was the perspective from which they viewed their suffering. They viewed their suffering from a *theocentric* (or God-centered) point of view, rather than an *anthropocentric* (man-centered) or *egocentric* (self-centered) point of view. These were men who saw themselves as servants of the

Most High God. They realized that they existed for God's glory and not the other way around. Hence, they rejoiced in their suffering. Their perspective may be foreign to some Christians in our culture, but bear with me as I attempt to explain.

First, allow me to say a word about the significance of this chapter because you may be asking yourself, "What does this have to do with anything?" Follow me. If our culture has adopted a post-Christian philosophy that embraces religious relativism, tolerance, and philosophical pluralism, and if biblical Christianity is completely at odds with such a philosophy, then there are two possible alternatives.

First, the culture can decide to be "neutral" and "balanced" toward biblical Christianity. We have already seen that these attitudes are not options. Second, our culture can continue to grow increasingly antagonistic toward biblical Christianity. The second alternative seems far more likely. That being the case, it is likely that the ease with which we have gone about our business will become a thing of the past. It is my prayer that the blood of Christian martyrs does not stain the streets of our cities, but it may, and in fact some argue that it already has.

In all likelihood, though, Christians will come under increasing cultural pressure, and we'll have some of our rights restricted. In any case, we must endure and overcome. If we are to do so, we must adopt a biblical perspective on suffering and trials.

A Lesson in the Air

On a recent trip home from a preaching engagement, I sat behind a father and his two- or three-year-old son. Mom was seated in the row ahead of them with two other children. As we began our descent into Houston's intercontinental airport, the boy began to cry. Any frequent flyer, or anyone who has ever flown with a small child, knows that the final approach can wreak havoc on a little one's ears.

As the plane descended, the boy's cries became more desperate. He held his ears and proclaimed to his father, "It hurts, Daddy! My ears hurt!" The man wrapped his arms around his son and told him, "Chew your gum, Buddy." The little boy would have none of it. He cried out again, "I don't want my gum." The man tried to explain to his son that chewing his gum would alleviate some of the pressure on his ears, but the boy simply could not understand.

In that little boy's mind, his father was being insensitive or at least unresponsive to his needs. As far as he knew, his father was changing the subject. I could imagine him thinking to himself, *I tell him my ears hurt, and he gives me gum? What's up with that?* I immediately thought of this chapter. I was watching one of the principles of it unfold before my very eyes. *The child does not always understand the father's instructions and/or responses in the midst of suffering.*

There are times when God's instruction to us seems completely irrelevant to our current condition. For instance, we struggle with our finances and meeting our bills, and what does God's Word teach us? Take the 100 percent that you are currently unable to make do with and give me 10 percent before you do anything else! What? If I can't make it on 100 percent, then how in the world will I survive on 90 percent? Nevertheless, if you have ever committed yourself to a lifestyle of giving, you know exactly what happens when you obey. God takes over and provides for your needs. It's simple. Our problem wasn't a lack of money but a lack of obedience that led to a lack of blessing. The answer is to obey and be blessed.

The reason many of us struggle with suffering is that we don't view it from the proper perspective. Our culture has painted a picture of suffering that places it outside the arena of Christian experience. We have somehow bought into the myth that belonging to Christ is the equivalent of purchasing a "get out of suffering free" card, but this belief is simply not true. The

Bible paints a picture of suffering that is quite different. In fact, the New Testament promises suffering to those who follow Christ.

Jesus on Suffering

Suffering does not equal lack of blessing.

One does not have to read far in the New Testament to find Jesus' teachings on Christians suffering for their faith. The Sermon on the Mount, Jesus' most popular sermon, begins in Matthew 5. In verse 4 he states, "Blessed are those who mourn, for they shall be comforted." Verses 11–12 make clear statements about Jesus' expectation for the treatment of his followers: "Blessed are you when people insult you and persecute you, and falsely say all kinds of evil against you because of Me. Rejoice and be glad, for your reward in heaven is great; for in the same way they persecuted the prophets who were before you." Normally, we would say, "We have never been persecuted. . . . The Lord has really blessed us." Here, however, the Lord says that those who have been persecuted are the ones who are blessed!

I am not arguing that people who have not seen persecution are not blessed. What I am saying is that suffering and persecution do not indicate the absence of the Lord's blessing in one's life.

Suffering is a by-product of identification with Christ.

My daughter Jasmine is a history buff. Recently, she has been fascinated with the plight of the Jews, Christians, gypsies, and others in Nazi Germany. As I write this chapter, she is reading about Corrie ten Boom. When she was eleven, she wrote a paper on Anne Frank. To aid her in her research, we took her to a Holocaust museum in St. Petersburg, Florida. It was a heartrending experience.

While we were looking at the pictures, my son, who was eight at the time, asked why the people in the pictures wore the stars on their clothing. I explained to him that the Jews were forced to wear these emblems as a means of identification. He looked perplexed, and then went on to ask, "Why didn't they just take them off?" If only it were that simple!

Those stars were merely symbols of the hatred of a regime whose goal was to eliminate all who were deemed unacceptable. All who did not fit the Nazi ideal were marked for extermination or deportation. This kind of hatred is almost unimaginable. In fact, some still deny it existed.

There is another regime bent on destroying undesirables. This regime is not political but spiritual. This regime is not led by Hitler but by Satan. He is the prince of the power of the air. He is the ruler of this world system. That is why one of the main causes of suffering in the life of a believer is his or her identification with Jesus. In fact, Jesus said: "If the world hates you, keep in mind that it hated me first. If you belonged to the world, it would love you as its own. As it is, you do not belong to the world, but I have chosen you out of the world. That is why the world hates you" (John 15:18–19 NIV).

Our identification with Christ is not marked by an emblem on our clothing but by the worldview we espouse and the manner in which we choose to live our lives. As long as we remain neutral and silent, we will be left alone. However, once we draw a line in the sand and align ourselves with the kingdom of God, the battle is on and we are in the fight.

Popularity is definitely overrated. Following Christ means turning one's back on the world. Why, then, would we ever expect to be accepted and applauded for our lifestyles? In fact, I get worried when I go too long without offending someone because of the choices I make or the opinions I voice. I know this sounds hard to believe!

This does not mean that we should go around attempting to offend people. On the contrary, it is our duty to avoid being unnecessarily offensive. For example, I would never walk around with a sign that says, "God hates fags," as some people do who claim to follow Christ. Such actions are an offense for the sake of being offensive. Besides that, the statement is not true. However, speaking the truth, even in love, is often offensive to a culture built upon a foundation of lies. Sometimes the people whom we offend most are those who claim to be Christians.

I have held full-time staff positions in four churches. The first two churches I served were black congregations. They were more than predominantly black; neither of them, to my knowledge, had even one white member. The third and fourth churches were predominantly white congregations with a handful of black, Hispanic, and Asian members. I knew they would be a challenge, but I was completely oblivious to the *kind* of opposition, ridicule, and criticism to which I was about to expose my family and myself.

It started almost immediately. "I never thought you would sell out," one family friend said. A family member asked my wife, "How can you stand to go to church with all those white people?" Several people asked me if I thought I was going to scar my children or if I realized the type of social damage we were inflicting upon them. Several black pastors commented, "It's a shame for one of our best and brightest young minds to be wasted on *them*." And of course there were the myriad accusations, both spoken and implied, that I was no more than a "token." All of these people, by the way, claimed to walk with Jesus!

Going to that third church was one of the most difficult transitions my family and I would ever undergo. We knew that God had called us to this place. We knew that we were involved in a historic event. However, the difficulty we anticipated was the cultural adaptation. We knew that this church would be unfamiliar territory and that we would be scrutinized. What we did not anticipate was the onslaught of "friendly fire." Amazing!

For decades men and women have lambasted white organizations for refusing to level the playing field for qualified blacks. There have been protests, marches, legislative efforts, trials, and immeasurable amounts of blood, sweat, tears, and even lives laid down in an effort to open closed doors. However, the moment I walked through one of those doors, those from whom I expected to hear sighs of relief and joyful cheers provided the only vocal opposition we encountered.

Suffering is part of the cost of discipleship.

Jesus affirmed this statement when he outlined the cost of following him. He stated, "If anyone wishes to come after me, he must deny himself, and take up his cross and follow Me" (Mark 8:34). This does not sound like an invitation to a life free of suffering. Indeed, Jesus was "a man of sorrows and acquainted with grief" (Isaiah 53:3). Why would anyone who follows him, then, expect to avoid suffering?

Anyone who has ever met a member of the United States Marine Corps knows that they pride themselves on being one of "The Few and the Proud." There is a note of pride in their voices as they inform their hearers that, unlike other branches of the military, they endure not eight, but thirteen weeks of basic training. "Our basic training is equivalent to the Army's basic training with special forces training tacked on," one Marine told me.

The challenge that Jesus issued to his disciples sounds a lot like a commercial for the Marine Corps. This was not a seeker-friendly, candy-coated, "warm fuzzy" designed to appease the faint of heart. On the contrary, Jesus' command was laying down the gauntlet; it was an invitation to count the cost and relinquish all rights to a life of comfort and leisure. As Dietrich Bonhoeffer wrote, "When Christ calls a man, he bids him come and die."[1]

Paul on Suffering

Suffering is temporal.

The Pauline view of suffering is not difficult to discover. Nor is it difficult to understand. In Romans 8:16–18 Paul offers this bold statement: "The Spirit Himself testifies with our spirit that we are children of God, and if children, heirs also, heirs of God and fellow heirs with Christ, if indeed we suffer with Him so that we may also be glorified with Him." Paul's assertion is virtually impossible to misinterpret, though some make a yeoman's effort. Paul views suffering as an integral element of the Christian life. However, he saw it as temporal.

Whatever we endure, it is not permanent. It is the proper understanding of this truth that has allowed believers to endure through the ages. I remember being taught as a child about Harriet Tubman and the famous Underground Railroad. I remember the stories of how the slaves in the fields would alert one another of the railroad's arrival by singing the old Negro spiritual, "Swing Low, Sweet Chariot."

However, as a young man without an understanding of the things of God, I had missed a very important part of the story. You see, the only reason "Swing Low" could be used in the fields to send coded messages about the Underground Railroad is that it was a common song among the slaves. The song was one of many that gave voice to the only source of hope that many slaves had—heaven.

In the midst of toil, turmoil, violence, inhumane treatment, and despair, there was a glimmer of hope—not just a hope that looked forward to freedom but a hope that looked forward to home. The words of the song speak for themselves:

I looked over Jordan and what did I see,
Comin' for to carry me home?
Was a band of angels comin' after me,
Comin' for to carry me home.

Swing low, sweet chariot,
Comin' for to carry me home,
Swing low, sweet chariot,
Comin' for to carry me home.

This song epitomizes a temporal view of suffering. No matter how bleak the circumstances, no matter how dark the night, a day is coming that will bring an end to our suffering and the dawn of a new day in a new home, the home for which we were made and in which we will finally find peace, comfort, and rest.

Suffering prepares believers to comfort others.

Listen to the familiarity with which Paul speaks of suffering to the Corinthian Christians: "Praise be to the God and Father of our Lord Jesus Christ, the Father of compassion and the God of all comfort, who comforts us in all our troubles, so that we can comfort those in any trouble with the comfort we ourselves have received from God" (2 Corinthians 1:3–4 NIV).

God uses the lessons learned through the suffering of one believer to comfort others. Also, the comfort that God supplies to his children in the midst of suffering serves to encourage those who witness this process. It creates an unseen bond between the one who has overcome and the one who is going through the suffering.

I sat riveted to the television during the week of September 11, 2001, as I watched the memorial services. I was struck by the way the family members shook hands, hugged, smiled, and cried on one another's shoulders. Some of these people may have met before, but many of them had never even been introduced. Yet there was an invisible bond between them. Each of them had gone through the same valley and without a word being spoken, they were able to say, "I understand."

All it takes is a simple phrase, "I've been where you are." Suddenly, a person in an immense struggle sees the value of this principle. There is nothing quite as encouraging as a comforting word from someone who has overcome the same difficulty.

Suffering is a means of strengthening and purifying faith.

In the summer of 2001, my family and I were tested. We had been living in England for a year while I finished up my doctoral studies at the University of Oxford. It had been a dream come true. My supervisors at Southeastern Seminary had agreed that I could finish my work abroad while I tested the waters to see if I wanted to stay at Oxford and work on a second doctoral degree (yes, I actually like school that much). In the end, we decided to return to the US, not because of the school but because my wife was miserable.

I thought she was just homesick. As it turned out, she was sick, all right, but not homesick. She had been in pain for about six months. She had complained but had never indicated how bad the pain really was. After several trips back to the doctor, we discovered that her body had been attacked by some very aggressive tumors. We were terrified! Bridget was thirty-five, and we didn't know if she was going to make it to thirty-six.

Over the next few months we experienced some of the most trying days of our lives. At times we prayed. At other times we cried. Yet there were days when we actually laughed. Our lives did not fall apart. We simply reminded ourselves of the times when God had shown himself real in our lives and declared our trust in him. This was not our first trial, and we knew it would not be our last.

Eventually, God used some great doctors to find and eliminate the tumors in my wife's body. She is completely whole. God again showed himself faithful. The trial made us stronger. Our faith in God and our love for each other grew immensely through our ordeal. We would never have experienced that kind of growth on the mountaintop. Therefore, "We also rejoice in our sufferings, because we know that suffering produces perseverance; perseverance, character; and character, hope" (Romans 5:3–4 NIV).

The writer's statement, "We also rejoice in our sufferings," is often taken out of context and misunderstood. It is not a "Thank you, sir, may I have another?" mentality. The truth expressed here is more akin to the attitude of an avid runner. When a runner says, "I love running," she does not necessarily mean, "I love the pounding of my feet against the pavement, the ache in my shins, and the burning in my chest." To the contrary, most runners don't like those things, or so runners tell me. What they do like, however, is the result these painful experiences bring. Thus, when they say, "I love running," we should hear, "I love keeping my weight under control; I love accomplishing personal goals; and I love taking care of my cardiovascular system." In other words, most runners actually love the results and benefits of running more than running itself.

The result is precisely what the apostle is attempting to communicate. We do not love suffering; we love the results that suffering brings. I did not enjoy those dark days, but I wouldn't trade them. I do not like to suffer, but I do want to grow and stretch my faith, and sometimes the only way that happens is for me to go through the valley of the shadow of death.

Jonathan Edwards was keenly aware of the purifying nature of trials. Edwards argued that there are at least three essential benefits of suffering and trials in the life of the believer. First, they reveal truth. Edwards wrote, "Trials tend to distinguish between what is true and what is false."[2] Next, according to Edwards, trials make faith more attractive. He wrote: "These trials, then, are a further benefit to true religion because they not only manifest its truth but they also enhance its genuine beauty and attractiveness. True virtue is loveliest when it is oppressed. The divine excellency of real Christianity is best exhibited when it is under the greatest trials."[3]

The third benefit of trials, according to Edwards, is that "they not only show [religion] to be true, they also free it from false admixtures."[4] He further states, "Nothing is left but that which is real. Trials enhance the attractiveness of true religion."[5]

To say that Jonathan Edwards had a different perspective on suffering and trials than do many Christians in our culture today would be a gross understatement. Edwards saw trials not only as inevitable but even as beneficial! This may seem strange, but it shouldn't. After all, this is the biblical view.

Suffering is an integral part of the Christian life.

The New Testament writers did not write about suffering as though it were not supposed to happen to Christians. On the contrary, Paul taught that this suffering is to be viewed not as an occasional occurrence but as a permanent part of the Christian life: "For just as the sufferings of Christ flow over into our lives, so also through Christ our comfort overflows. If we are distressed, it is for your comfort and salvation; if we are comforted, it is for your comfort, which produces in you patient endurance of the same sufferings we suffer. And our hope for you is firm, because we know that just as you share in our sufferings, so also you share in our comfort" (2 Corinthians 1:5–7 NIV).

Many Christians in our culture have had such limited experience with suffering that this sounds morbid. But think of it this way: What if a professional football team went through an entire season without experiencing one injury? One way the team could view this turn of events is to say, "We were truly blessed this season." Another way they could respond is to say, "I guess injuries should no longer be viewed as a normal part of the game of football." Of course the latter is completely unreasonable. Anyone who knows the game of football knows that teams don't make it through a game, let alone a season, without some degree of injury.

The modern American view of suffering resembles the aforementioned scenario. Many Christians have gone through life having been convinced that we are supposed to go through our lives without suffering. Thus, when difficulties of any sort arise in their lives, they immediately cry out to God, "How could you let this happen?" On the other hand, if we viewed suffering from the biblical perspective, as inevitable for the Christian as injuries are in football, our response would be entirely different.

I am not suggesting that we become oblivious to suffering. That is unreasonable. I am suggesting, however, that we stop acting like it is not part of the game and an essential part at that.

Suffering is part of our preparation for glory.

Perhaps the most famous passage about suffering in Paul's writings is found in Philippians 3:7–11:

But whatever was to my profit I now consider loss
for the sake of Christ. What is more, I consider everything a loss compared to the surpassing greatness of
knowing Christ Jesus my Lord, for whose sake I have
lost all things. I consider them rubbish, that I may
gain Christ and be found in him, not having a righteousness of my own that comes from the law, but that
which is through faith in Christ—the righteousness
that comes from God and is by faith. I want to know
Christ and the power of his resurrection and the fellowship of sharing in his sufferings, becoming like
him in his death, and so, somehow, to attain to the
resurrection from the dead (NIV).

Nowhere is Paul's view of the inevitability of suffering more evident than in 2 Timothy. In fact, you can't go an entire chapter in 2 Timothy without running into a reference to suffering or persecution! Keep in mind, this is a letter written by a man in prison who is fully aware that he is about to be put to death. In fact, he is about to be executed for preaching the gospel, and he takes the time to encourage his young protégé to continue to do just that. The following synopsis emphasizes Paul's teachings on suffering.

Chapter 1

"Do not be ashamed of the testimony of our Lord, or of me His *prisoner*" (v. 8).
"That is why I am *suffering* as I am" (v. 12 NIV).

Chapter 2

"*Suffer hardship* with me as a good soldier of Christ Jesus" (v. 3).

Chapter 3

"Realize this, that in the last days *difficult* times will come (v. 1).
"You followed my teaching, conduct, purpose, faith, patience, love, perseverance, *persecutions and sufferings*" (vv. 10–11).
"Indeed, all who desire to live godly in Christ Jesus will be *persecuted*" (v. 12).

Chapter 4

"But you, be sober in all things, *endure hardship*, do the work of an evangelist" (v. 5).
Just a cursory overview of 2 Timothy reveals that any view of Christianity that does not include suffering is inconsistent with the view Paul presents.

Peter on Suffering

Suffering is a tool God uses to shape his children.

Perhaps the most exigent New Testament statement about suffering comes from Peter. In chapter 4 of his first epistle he says: "Dear friends, do not be surprised at the painful trial you are suffering, as though something strange were happening to you. But rejoice that you participate in the sufferings of Christ, so that you may be overjoyed when his glory is revealed. If you are insulted because of the name of Christ, you are blessed, for the Spirit of glory and of God rests on you. If you suffer, it should not be as a murderer or thief or any other kind of criminal, or even as a meddler. However, if you suffer as a Christian, do not be ashamed, but praise God that you bear that name" (1 Peter 4:12–16 NIV).

Again, there is little need for comment. The Scripture is clear; suffering is not foreign to true followers of Christ.

A. W. Tozer said, "It is doubtful whether God can use a man greatly unless he hurt him deeply."[6] You may not believe that, but ask yourself a question: Have you ever met or read about a believer whose walk with God you found inspiring, even intimidating, whose life was not littered with trials? I can honestly say that I have not. Every believer whom I have come to respect and look up to has had immense trials to overcome.

I am convinced that the mountaintop is the place we celebrate, but the valley is the place we learn. In many ways our Christian life is like a tube of toothpaste—you don't really know what's in there until you squeeze. When we are squeezed, we see where we are in our walk. If we are squeezed and the result is a worldly response, we know that we have a long way to go. But if the response is an unexplainable reflection of the Savior, we know that we are being conformed to his image.

A quick glance at the men and women whom God has used throughout history reveals the truth of this principle. Charles Spurgeon, the pastor of London's great Metropolitan Tabernacle, was considered the prince of preachers. Few people realize, though, that Spurgeon's wife was an invalid for many years and that his own health was so poor that he spent summers on continental Europe seeking treatment.

Fannie Crosby, the famous hymn writer who penned "Pass Me Not, O Gentle Savior" and many other beloved songs of the faith, was blind. The prominent Great Awakening preacher George Whitefield would sometimes spit up blood while he preached. The beloved missionary Lottie Moon battled illness throughout much of her life.

Suffering as a Call to Repentance

In other instances suffering is part of a process designed to draw us away from our sin and back to God. We love to quote 2 Chronicles 7:14: "If my people, who are called by my name, will humble themselves and pray and seek my face and turn from their wicked ways, then will I hear from heaven and will forgive their sin and will heal their land." We seem to forget that verse 13 precedes this passage: "When I shut up the heavens so that there is no rain, or command locusts to devour the land or send a plague among my people." God disciplines his people. He makes this clear when he says, "Those whom I love, reprove and discipline" (Revelation 3:19).

I love my children. Sometimes, however, I am called upon to discipline them. In those instances my children do not always understand. I remember one instance when my son demonstrated his lack of understanding in this area. My son had disobeyed his mother, and I sent him to my office.

When I told him to wait for me there, he looked up at me and said, "You mean to my room?" "No," I replied, "I mean to my office." He knew that if I sent him to his room, I would want him to sit and think about what he had done. Perhaps he would have to write a paragraph about his bad behavior and what the Lord would have had him do differently. Perhaps he would have to write an apology to his mother and read it aloud, but the office. That is where we keep the "board of education"!

Make no mistake about it. Sometimes the suffering that we endure is akin to a spanking from God. I am in no way implying that our sin debt is anything but paid in full. In order to grasp this, we must understand that the only means by which a person is saved is the finished work of Jesus Christ on the cross. As the Reformers echoed, "We are saved by grace alone, through faith alone, in Christ alone."

Let me be clear. I am not suggesting that we pay for our own sin; Christ did that. Nor am I suggesting that God is a scornful judge who sits on high waiting for us to mess up so he can rap us across the knuckles. Nothing could be further from the truth. Our God is a benevolent, loving, patient Father who loves his children deeply. What I am suggesting is that our Father does not always rescue us from the consequences of our behavior.

For example, there are Christians who have gone to jail because they broke the law. There are also Christians who only get to see their children every other weekend and six weeks in the summer because they broke their marriage vows. There are Christians who flunked out of college because they wasted their time and talents. In these cases and others like them, God does allow believers to suffer the consequences of their sin.

Just imagine the alternative. If God did not allow sinning believers to suffer the consequences, at least three aspects of the Christian faith would be fundamentally and irrevocably changed. First, the decision to come to Christ would be clouded by a desire for a consequence-free life. Many people, seeing the lives of Christians and realizing that they got away with everything, would come running to Christ, not for forgiveness of sin but for relief from sin's consequences!

The second thing that would change would be the complete removal of all accountability in the lives of Christians. The man who cheats on his wife would never be found out. The child who lies and steals would never get caught. The pastor whose life is inconsistent with the righteous requirements of his office would never be discovered. Holiness and sanctification would be meaningless words.

Third, and most important, God's character would be violated. The fact of the matter is, God allows the rain to fall on the just and the unjust. If God removes the consequences of a person's sin in order to demonstrate his sovereignty or to accomplish another goal, he is being merciful. However, if God removes the consequences of every believer's sin, he is not acting according to his revealed character. If a Christian drinks and drives and God shows him or her mercy and they neither hurt another person nor go to jail but instead gain victory over their sin and tell others of God's goodness, then God has mercifully used their sin for his glory. However, if God only allows non-Christians to have wrecks and get arrested as a result of their sin in this area, the rain is no longer falling on both the just and the unjust.

Suffering as a Means of Building a Testimony

Sometimes the purpose of our suffering is not just our growth or even our identification with Christ. Sometimes the purpose of our suffering is the story we get to tell. Nothing speaks more powerfully to our faith in Christ than our attitude toward the trials in our lives.

John 9:1–5 illustrates how God sometimes uses our suffering in this way. Jesus and his disciples encounter a man who was born blind. His disciples ask, "Rabbi, who sinned, this man or his parents, that he was born blind?" This question betrayed their theological inclination to view all suffering as a direct result of personal sin. Jesus, however, had a different explanation. He said, "Neither this man nor his parents sinned, but this happened so that the work of God might be displayed in his life."

Did you catch that? This man was blind so that God could heal him. Moreover, this healing was designed to display the glory of God and validate the ministry of the Messiah. This man had suffered his whole life! He had never seen the light of day;

he had never looked into the eyes of his mother; he had never watched children play or birds fly south for the winter. His had been, in the eyes of many, a miserable existence.

All of that changed, however, with one encounter. He met Jesus and was healed. For the first time in his life he could see. What a testimony! But without the suffering there would have been no testimony. God is in the business of turning our trials into testimonies. This is not to say that God caused the blindness for the sake of the testimony. The fact is that we live in a fallen, imperfect world filled with sin, sickness, and disease. God, however, occasionally steps in and shows himself tangibly in the lives of those who will trust him.

I saw this in an unforgettable way during a pastoral visit to a hospital a few years ago. I was headed to the M. D. Anderson Cancer Center in Houston. I knew that the person I was about to visit was very sick. Upon closer examination I recognized the name and realized that the woman I was about to call upon (I will call her Gloria) was in the terminal stages of the disease.

I rehearsed my words in my mind. I wanted to make sure that I was sensitive to God's Spirit as I walked into the room. When I arrived, Gloria was not there. I asked the nurse where she had gone, and she looked at me and said, "She's gone." Immediately I knew what she meant. Gloria had died. But that was only part of the story.

The nurse and I talked for a few moments, and she recounted Gloria's last few moments. I was overwhelmed by the story the nurse told. This young woman, whose life ended prematurely in our eyes, did not fight death; she embraced it. The impact on the nurse was obvious. She said, "I have never seen anyone go like that." At the end of that conversation, I stood there and soaked it all in. In that moment God showed me something that I will never forget: Sometimes God is glorified when sick saints get well. Other times God is glorified when sick saints *die* well. This woman's death was a testimony. She said more by the way she embraced her trial, and eventually her death, than many believers say in their health and prosperity.

This chapter is far from an exhaustive treatment of the idea of suffering in the New Testament. Such a treatment would be a book in itself. My goal is simply to demonstrate that suffering is not, as some teach, a concept foreign to the Christian experience. This being said, the suffering that believers endure always has a purpose. God does not allow his children to suffer needlessly.

Section Three

What Shall We Say?

Immediately following the Civil War, special riders were dispatched and sent to plantations throughout the South. These riders had what I consider an enviable task. They would ride from plantation to plantation, informing slaves of Lincoln's Emancipation Proclamation, which brought them their freedom. The response of the slaves varied. Some cried and cheered, but others refused to believe the news and returned to work. Still others stood in stunned silence. Nevertheless, the fact remained: they were free.

I have often tried to imagine what it must have felt like to be one of those slaves. I imagine the feeling of exhilaration, which must have been followed by great fear. *What will we do?* many thought. *Are they really going to let us go?* I have also imagined what it would have felt like to be one of those previously freed riders. What a great honor it must have been to look into the eyes of men and women, most of whom had never tasted freedom, and tell them slavery was history!

I have had the privilege of being on both sides of that fence. No, I have never been a slave to men, but I was a slave to sin. I was lost and without hope until Jesus set me free. I remember the face of the man who informed me of my spiritual emancipation. I have also had the privilege of being on the other side, where God has granted me the distinguished honor of delivering the news to a captive who was about to be set free. I pray that every believer who reads this book will have that honor. We must realize however, that it will not happen if we are content to sit on the sidelines and watch others carry the news.

Thus far, we have examined two inevitable realities. The first reality is that the culture we live in stands in opposition to the truth upon which we base our existence. The second reality is that the truth which is our foundation demands that we resist and impact our culture. The next logical question is, "What shall we say?" Section 3 offers an answer to that question.

8

WHY BELIEVE
THE BIBLE?

The next two chapters put forth evidences for the historicity and veracity of the Bible and the Christian view of Jesus. These evidences serve at least two purposes. These evidences serve to convince us so that we can passionately defend the claims of Christ. It is essential that those of us who claim to follow Christ be thoroughly equipped with a working knowledge of the Bible and of Christ if we are to stand in the face of the Sanhedrin of our day. Second, these evidences serve to convince us that we can always be ready "to make a defense to everyone who asks you to give an account for the hope that is in you" (1 Peter 3:15). The word "defense" (*apologia*) can be translated "a reasoned response." This is more than just stating, "That's just the way I was raised to believe!"

I am not suggesting that the Bible needs our help. On the contrary, I tend to agree with Charles Haddon Spurgeon, who said that the Bible is like a lion. You don't have to help a lion; "just turn him loose." I do, however, believe that it is important for us to learn to reason from the Scriptures as Paul did in Thessalonica (Acts 17:2). Knowing how to do so is especially necessary in the intellectual climate in which we live.

One of the main premises upon which religious relativism operates is that all holy books are created equal. To the relativist, it does not matter whether one reads the Bible, the Book of Mormon, or the Qur'an; they are all man-made books that contain good teachings, but none of them can make an exclusive claim on the truth. Many Christians, however, believe that the Bible is the Word of God and contains truth without any mixture of error.

Of course, many would argue that such sentiment is the result of "blind faith" or ignorance. In fact, an Oxford professor accused me of believing the Bible in favor of other books simply because I grew up with that worldview. He went on to state, "Had you grown up in India, you would have believed the Hindu faith." Imagine his utter shock when I informed him that my mother had in fact practiced Buddhism when I was a young man and that I had never heard the message of the gospel until my freshman year of college! Over the next several minutes, I was able to explain the foundation upon which my belief in the Bible was based.

A Reliable Collection of Historical Documents

Peter writes, "We did not follow cleverly invented stories when we told you about the power and coming of our Lord Jesus Christ" (2 Peter 1:16). The implication is that the Bible is not a collection of myths but a collection of historical documents. The Bible is not a mere story like the Gilgamesh Epic; it is history! Luke makes this same assertion when he writes: "Many have undertaken to draw up an account of the things that have been fulfilled among us, just as they were handed down to us by those who from the first were eyewitnesses and servants of the word. Therefore, since I myself have carefully investigated everything from the beginning, it seemed good also to me to write an orderly account for you, most excellent

Theophilus, so that you may know the certainty of the things you have been taught" (Luke 1:1-4 NIV).

Historical veracity is a very important point in light of opposition to the historicity of the Bible. One of the most consistent objections levied against the Bible is the fact that it was written by men.

You may have heard it stated, "Why should I believe the Bible? It was written by men, and anything written by men must be flawed." Notice two problems with this argument. First, this argument overlooks the fact that the Bible claims to have been written by men under God's influence. Second, to believe this argument, one would be forced to disregard every historical fact one has ever read in a book. After all, humans have written every history book, every math book, every science book, and every other kind of book. Imagine a student standing up in her math class and proclaiming, "I cannot believe the Pythagorean theorem because it came from a book written by a man!" How ridiculous! Nevertheless, this is a consistent indictment against the Bible.

The question is not whether men wrote any book, but whether the information contained in that book is accurate and reliable. The reason we believe the Pythagorean theorem is that it works! The reason we believe a history book is that it is consistent with evidence and corroborated by other accounts. In fact, we often believe history books without such evidence. No one questions the validity of information based upon the fact that it is contained in a book written by a man or woman. Nor should we question the content of the Bible. The question should be, "Do we have reliable historical information?" And the answer is a resounding yes.

Five main arguments support the historicity of the Bible. First, the Bible comes from varied, yet consistent sources. Second, there is an abundance of early copies of the biblical texts. Third, the Bible was translated into other languages very soon after being compiled. Fourth, the writings of the early church fathers contain massive quotations of the biblical texts. Fifth, the Bible is corroborated by archeological evidence. Let's take a closer look at each of these pieces of evidence.

Varied but Consistent Sources

The Bible was written in three different languages: Hebrew, Aramaic, and Greek. This in itself is an astounding fact. I speak English, as well as some Spanish, and I know how hard it is to think about simple concepts in two different languages. Imagine finding consistent, coherent thought flowing through a document that came from three language sources!

Furthermore, the Bible was written on three separate continents: Asia, Africa, and Europe, but the message is the same throughout. Imagine the likelihood of finding consistency of thought in such a collection of documents! My family and I recently visited New York. I absolutely loved it! I know people are often put off by the city's size and crowds, but I had so much fun that I remarked to my wife, "I could be a New Yorker." Nevertheless, it did not take long to realize that we weren't in Texas anymore. The city had an entirely different set of rules. On more than one occasion, I opened the door for ladies who chose to open another door for themselves instead. I also spoke to several people on the street who looked at me like I was from the moon (or Texas). I was definitely in a different culture. And New York and Texas are in the same country—not to mention on the same continent.

The Bible was also written by more than forty different authors, most of whom never knew one another. They were people from different cultures, different times, and different backgrounds. Moses was royalty, Joshua was a military general, David was first a shepherd and then a king, Amos was a fig farmer, Peter was a fisherman, and Matthew was a tax collector. What an awkward collaboration!

Finally, the Bible was written over a period of approximately sixteen hundred years. This is more astounding than the idea of traversing languages and geographical barriers. The changes within a single culture or language over the course of a generation can be overwhelming, but the changes in multiple cultures and multiple languages over a period of one and a half millennia are almost unfathomable. This span of time, however, is the backdrop of the Bible.

Astoundingly, this collection of documents from three continents, written in three languages, by more than forty different authors, over a period of sixteen hundred years has one single theme and purpose: the creation, fall and redemption of humanity for the glory of God.

In the next few segments, as we look at the remaining four arguments for the Bible's historical veracity and authenticity, we will turn our attention to the text of the New Testament. I will not attempt to ignore the Old Testament documents (to which we will return), but I will make an effort to answer the most common objections raised by skeptics. The next chapter is devoted to the person and work of Jesus Christ, and the following sections of this chapter will serve as foundations for some of the arguments made there.

Abundance of Early Biblical Text Copies

Over five thousand Greek manuscripts contain all or part of the New Testament. The earliest copies we currently have can be dated as early as the first half of the second century, earlier than the year A.D. 150.[1] The dating of the documents is often discouraging to believers who are not familiar with ancient documents. In fact, some skeptics argue that documents written decades after the events which they record offer little compelling evidence—that is, until they compare the New Testament documents to other writings from antiquity.

For example, Julius Caesar's *Gallic Wars* stands virtually unchallenged in regard to its authenticity and historicity, in spite of the fact that we have only approximately ten manuscripts of these writings, the earliest of which is dated approximately nine hundred years after Caesar's death. Aristotle's *Poetics* is another classic. There are approximately five portions of this document available today, the earliest of which was written fourteen hundred years after the life of Aristotle. Again, these documents are rarely challenged.

These are some of the best examples history has to offer. However, when compared to the text of the New Testament for historicity and authenticity, they do not belong in the same class. I often compare them to a baby in a bodybuilding competition—the comparison is that overwhelming.

Early Translation into Multiple Languages

Before Jesus ascended to his Father, he left his apostles with some final instructions. The most famous of these is the Great Commission (Matthew 28:19–20). Jesus told his followers to go and make disciples of *ta ethnē*, which literally means "every people group." This was a monumental task. Especially when you consider that with multiple people groups came multiple languages. Therefore, if the gospel message was going to be spread abroad, it first had to be translated.

This translation process gives us one of the most compelling pieces of evidence for the authenticity and historicity of the Bible. Documents that were translated into other languages could be traced back to their source. Further, if the date of their translation is known, they can be used to establish the authenticity of earlier source documents. To the novice, this process may seem boring, but trust me, this is exciting stuff!

Let's imagine that I write a poem addressed to my wife, Bridget. Eventually, the overwhelming beauty and depth of this poem is too much for Bridget to keep to herself, so she shares it with her sister, Pam. Pam is moved to tears. (Now don't laugh at the idea of my poetry being that good!) In fact, Pam is so moved that she makes a copy for herself and returns the original to Bridget. Eventually, Pam, overwhelmed by the beauty and passion of the poem, makes copies for all of her friends. One of her friends, Patrice, happens to be an international flight attendant who frequently flies to Spain and Portugal. This flight attendant is seen crying on one of her flights, prompting a passenger to ask, in broken English, "Why are you crying?" The passenger reads the poem and is utterly astonished by its magnificence. "I must write this in my language," the passenger exclaims, fighting back his emotions.

Now we have an international, multilingual poem traveling all over the world. Eventually the poem is published in twenty languages. A historian finds the original letter fifty years from now. He discovers a Chinese version and traces it back to its origins. Then by tracing the name *Bridget*, he discovers the language of origin. Ultimately, his diligence pays off, and he finds one of the copies written down by Pam, the second recipient. Through comparisons of her handwriting he is able to find several of the copies she made. Eventually, he is able to recreate the document in its original form and compare any translation for accuracy. He can also accurately date the source material, and by investigating Pam's life, he can find her sister, Bridget, and me, the author who touched the world with the depth, passion, and beauty of the original poem. (It could happen!)

As you can see, translations have great historical benefits. Translations of the New Testament documents are of great worth in establishing the authenticity and historicity of the New Testament documents. In his book *The Text of the New Testament*, Bruce Metzger states, "The earliest versions of the New Testament were prepared by missionaries to assist in the propagation of the Christian faith among peoples whose native tongue was Syriac, Latin, or Coptic."[2]

One of the Syriac versions was possibly translated as early as the third century. This is a crucial point, considering that many people argue for very late writing of the New Testament. Such late dating is impossible when viewed in light of such early translations. To go back to our illustration, that would be like our researcher finding my poem fifty years after it was written and arguing that it had only been written five years earlier, when there are translations of the original poem in other languages that are more than forty years old. This is exactly what people do when they attribute the writings of the New Testament to first-century ghost writers or fourth- and fifth-century monks— but more about this theory later.

Writings of the Church Fathers

Have you ever watched one of those "World's Funniest" or "World's Dumbest" video shows? I love to look at those programs and laugh. It is amazing what some people will do when they think no one is watching! I vividly remember one show about a crook and a video camera. The crook had broken into a store and begun to rob the place. He and his accomplice methodically went through the store taking the most valuable items they could find. Then it happened! One of the men spotted the security camera.

What happened next would have been hysterical if it weren't so sad. The crooks began to beat and pull at the camera until they tore it out of the ceiling. They then took the camera away in order to avoid leaving any evidence. However, there was one problem—they left the tape. Everything they had done was recorded on tape, and they were eventually identified and caught. Removing the camera meant absolutely nothing.

What, you may ask, do these thieves' actions have to do with the writings of the early church fathers? The church fathers acted as a sort of taping device used in preserving the Scriptures. They wrote letters, sermons, commentaries, and jou nals in which they painstakingly copied passages of Scripture. In fact, Metzger comments, "So extensive are these citations that if all other sources for our knowledge of the text of the New Testament were destroyed, they would be sufficient alone for the reconstruction of practically the entire New Testament."[3]

I love to point this out to people who argue that the Bible has been changed over the years by zealous monks trying to cover up inconsistencies. This type of behavior would be as dumb as removing a video camera without taking the tape. First, we would have to ignore the fact that there are over five thousand Greek manuscripts and that any monk wishing to change the Bible would have to collect at least a majority of them. Second, this zealous monk would have to make sure that all of the early translations were gathered and destroyed. Third, he would have to eliminate the writings of the early church fathers, and finally, he would have to single-handedly spread his doctored documents throughout the world, returning them to the museums, monasteries, churches, and individual collections from which he stole them. Please! That would be a bigger feat than parting the Red Sea!

The zealous-monk theory is ludicrous. There are layers of textual evidence that simply cannot be ignored. The biblical text was written early and copied often. Further, the text was translated into multiple languages and spread throughout the world. Add to this the fact that those who read the early texts quoted and cited them so extensively that they virtually reproduced them again. All this adds up to a mountain of evidence that can only be ignored by those with a predilection to do so.

Archaelogical (Eyewitness) Corroboration

In addition to being well documented, the historicity and authenticity of the Bible is bolstered by the fact that it was written by eyewitnesses. Peter wrote, "but we were eyewitnesses of His majesty" (2 Peter 1:16b). These were not stories that were passed down from generation to generation; these were first-hand accounts. Listen to the repetitive emphasis in 1 John 1–3: "That which was from the beginning, which we have *heard*, which we have *seen with our eyes*, which we have *looked at* and *our hands have touched*—this we proclaim concerning the Word of life. The life *appeared*; we have *seen it* and testify to it, and we proclaim to you the eternal life, which was with the Father and *has appeared* to us. We proclaim to you what we have *seen and heard*, so that you also may have fellowship with us. And our fellowship is with the Father and with his Son, Jesus Christ" (NIV).

John went to great lengths to establish the eyewitness nature of his account. Note the use of sensory language (*seen, heard, touched*). Also, note the repetitive nature of the verbs: He uses *heard* two times, *seen* or *looked at* four times, and *appeared* two times. The author is attempting to establish and reiterate the firsthand nature of his testimony. He, like most of the New Testament writers, had seen the risen Christ firsthand.

I was a student at Southwestern Seminary during the O. J. Simpson trials. On the day the verdict came down, I was standing in a room in the administrative offices watching this historic moment unfold. The verdict was read: Not guilty. Suddenly, there were two distinct outbursts, one from disgusted white students, the other from elated blacks. I found myself watching students and faculty more than I was watching the television. I was amazed by the distinct reaction of both groups. But why was there such a distinction?

Many sociologists have argued that black people responded to the verdict out of a visceral reaction to injustice in the past. On the other hand, most white Americans had far more faith in the judicial system and believed that the LAPD and the district attorney would never have brought a fraudulent case against Simpson simply because they did not like the fact that he was a black man who had been married to a white woman.

I don't know how true either assumption was, but I do know that it was precisely the explanation that I received from scores of people, both black and white. Neither group was satisfied. Those who considered Simpson guilty wished that Mark Fuhrman had crawled under a rock somewhere instead of showing up at the scene. Those who believed in Simpson's innocence wished that he had better taste in shoes and a better explanation for the cut on his hand. In either case, though, a few eyewitnesses would have made all the difference.

Imagine the reaction to the verdict if several people had seen Simpson during the time of the murders or had seen him commit the crimes. There would have been little doubt in anyone's mind. Eyewitness evidence would have been more powerful than prejudice on either side. Those convinced of Simpson's guilt would not possibly have been so certain if he had thrown a dinner party that night and had been entertaining guests until he got into the limo to leave for the airport. And those convinced of his innocence would not have maintained their allegiance if two or three people who had never met one another and who had no connection to O. J. or the LAPD had taken the stand and recounted the same story of how they had seen him commit the murder.

There is nothing more powerful than corroborated eyewitness accounts, which is precisely what we have in the case of the authenticity and historicity of the resurrection of Jesus. John saw Jesus; so did Peter and James and Matthew. These were eyewitnesses who corroborated one another's stories. Contrast the disciples' strikingly similar accounts to the claims of Joseph Smith or the Prophet Muhammad, both of whom told stories of special revelations to which no other person was privy. This in and of itself does not negate the possibility that Smith and Muhammad told the truth, but lack of eyewitness testimony does make their stories more difficult to believe.

A Reliable Collection of Supernatural Events

So far we have established only that the Bible is a good history book. However, it goes far beyond mere history. The Bible contains firsthand accounts of miracles! Thus, we must expand our definition: *The Bible is a reliable collection of historical documents, written by eyewitnesses who report the occurrence of supernatural events.*

Peter goes on to write, "For he received honor and glory from God the Father when the voice came to him from the Majestic Glory, saying, 'This is my Son, whom I love; with him I am well pleased.' We ourselves heard this voice that came from heaven when we were with him on the sacred mountain" (2 Peter 1:17–18 NIV). The mountain Peter writes of is the Mount of Transfiguration, where the disciples had witnessed not only the transfiguration of Jesus but also the appearance of Moses and Elijah. At this point Peter's argument leaves the realm of mere history and enters the realm of divine revelation.

For some people, stories of similar supernatural events are all they need to close the book on the issue of the validity of the Bible. I can't tell you how many times I have heard, "I can believe the teachings of Jesus, but the miracles are a little far-fetched." In fact, many so-called Christian scholars have taken a similar position. They simply deny the supernatural aspects of the Bible in an effort to maintain intellectual integrity. The only problem with this approach is that their efforts are not based on scholarship but on prejudice and presupposition.

One of the strongest of the presuppositions applied to the denial of the supernatural events of the Bible is the aforementioned philosophy called naturalism. Naturalism is a belief that nature is a closed system and that the supernatural cannot exist. Operating under such an assumption would demand the a priori exclusion of all miracles.

A Record of Events That Fulfill Specific Prophecies

Not only does the Bible report the occurrence of supernatural events, but these events often took place as fulfillment of specific prophecies given beforehand. Hence, we need an even more expanded definition: *The Bible is a collection of historical documents, written by eyewitnesses who reported the occurrence of supernatural events, which took place as fulfillment of specific prophecy.* Peter's argument continues, "So we have the prophetic word made more sure" (2 Peter 1:19a). Peter is not writing of the previous uncertainty of prophecy but to the fact that, in Christ, those prophecies are fulfilled. The following chart lists events in Jesus' life that specifically fulfill Old Testament prophecies:

EVENT IN JESUS' LIFE	OT PROPHECY	NT FULFILLMENT
Born in Bethlehem	Micah 5:2	Luke 2:4–7
Born of a virgin	Isaiah 7:14	Luke 1:26–38
Sold for thirty silver pieces	Zechariah 1:13	Matthew 26:15
Silver used to buy field	Zechariah 11:13	Matthew 27:6
Mocked during death	Psalm 22:7	Matthew 27:27–32
Condemned with criminals	Psalm 22:15	John 19:28
Silent when accused	Isaiah 53:7	Matthew 27:12–14
Pierced hands and feet	Psalm 22:16	John 19:18
Pierced after death	Isaiah 53:5	Luke 23:46
Lots cast for his clothes	Psalm 22:18	John 19:23–25
Buried by a rich man	Isaiah 53:9	Matthew 27:57–60
Resurrection	Psalm 16:10	John 20:11–18

While there are several instances of fulfilled prophecy in the life of Jesus, the one place to which I continually return is Psalm 22. The astounding relevance of this passage of Scripture begins with its first line. Had Jesus wished to draw an audience's attention to what we now call Psalm 22, he would simply have referred to the psalm by its first line: "My God, My God, why have You forsaken me?" If this line sounds familiar, it is because these are the very words Jesus spoke while he was on the cross. He could just as well have been saying, "Open your scrolls to Psalm 22."

Since the Psalms were actual songs known throughout Hebrew culture, hearers would certainly have been aware of at least some of the lines in the text. They would have remembered, for example, the psalmist's words: "All those who see me mock me; they hurl insults, shaking their heads: 'He trusts in the LORD; let the LORD rescue him. Let him deliver him, since he delights in him'" (vv. 7–8 NIV).

The tension must have been palpable when people realized that these statements were being made during the crucifixion they were witnessing. Imagine hearing someone shout at Jesus while he is gasping for air and struggling for every breath. Someone from the crowd says, "He saved others; let Him save Himself if He is the Christ of God" (Luke 23:35).

In addition to recognizing the mockery, those who heard Jesus' outcry would have been reminded of the psalm's prophecy of crucifixion by Gentiles and hanging between evil men (v. 16). Imagine the astonishment of a faithful Jew or God-fearing person as he or she watched the verbal exchange between Jesus and the two transgressors with whom he was executed. The sound of the nails being driven into Jesus' hands and feet must have rung in the ears of those who recalled the psalmist's words, "They pierced my hands and my feet" (v. 16).

These are specific, detailed prophecies of the crucifixion, made a thousand years before Jesus was born. What's more, these prophecies were made by a man who never once saw a crucifixion in his life because crucifixion had not yet been invented.

The prophets not only mentioned the coming of the Messiah, but they also made statements about issues that affect the world today. For example, Ezekiel 26 has a detailed account of the destruction of the city of Tyre. This in itself is astonishing considering the fact that the city fell just as it had been foretold, destroyed by Nebuchadnezzar and later Alexander the Great. Even more astonishing, however, is the fact that the prophet clearly states that the city will *never* be rebuilt. To this day, the city of Tyre lies in ruins in spite of numerous attempts to reconstruct it.

A Record of Changed Lives

One of the strongest pieces of evidence supporting the authenticity of the Bible is the manner in which it impacts the lives of those who earnestly read it. Hence, *The Bible is a life-changing collection of historical documents, written by eyewitnesses who reported the occurrence of supernatural events, which took place as fulfillment of specific prophecies.*

Peter uses a phrase that is one of the most difficult statements in the Bible. He refers to the Bible as a book to which "you do well to pay attention as to a light shining in a dark place, until the day dawns and the morning star arises in your hearts" (2 Peter 1:19). I don't pretend to know the background of this statement. Many scholars speculate as to the first-century figure of speech to which Peter is referring, but few seem convinced. There is little doubt, however, that it refers to the Bible's impact on the lives of its readers.

What I find interesting about this section of Peter's argument *is* its location. He did not start by saying, "The Bible is true because it changed my life," as some are apt to do. He began with evidence authenticating the Bible, then he added the personal touch as if to say, "And besides all that, it is alive and active and changes lives and cultures." This balance is crucial. My personal testimony is no substitute for the evidence of the Bible's authenticity, but the evidence is no substitute for my testimony. The two work hand in hand.

On the one hand my testimony cannot stand without a foundation, as I have demonstrated in chapter 5. Everyone has a testimony. The drug addict who got off drugs because he made the lamppost in front of his house his "higher power" has a testimony of genuine life change. However, his testimony does not change the fact that the lamppost did absolutely nothing, and is in fact no more than a lamppost.

On the other hand, a sound, logical, philosophical argument for the authenticity of biblical documents without real-world evidence of effectual change would be useless. Imagine a drug company putting out an ad that read, "Use Cure-All, the new fast-acting, pain-relieving, antiaging wonder drug that will cure whatever ails you. We've never tested it, but our research indicates it should work." While there are hypochondriacs out there who would line up to use this new product, most people would turn the other way. Not many want to trust their health to unproven drugs. By the same token, no one wants to trust his soul to an unproven faith. People want to know that it works, not only in theory but also in practice.

A Book with Divine Origins

On the issue of the Bible's origins, Peter writes: "Above all, you must understand that no prophecy of Scripture came about by the prophet's own interpretation. For prophecy never had its origin in the will of man, but men spoke from God as they were carried along by the Holy Spirit" (2 Peter 1:20–21 NIV). Peter identifies the crux of the matter. God is the author of the Bible.

Our final definition is this: *The Bible is a life-changing collection of historical documents, written by eyewitnesses who reported the occurrence of supernatural events; these events took place as fulfillment of specific prophecy, and point to the Bible's divine origins.*

One of the most poignant statements of this reality is in Paul's second letter to Timothy: "All Scripture is God-breathed and is useful for teaching, rebuking, correcting and training in righteousness, so that the man of God may be thoroughly equipped for every good work" (2 Timothy 3:16–17 NIV).

The writer of Hebrews makes it clear that this inspiration is consistent throughout both the Old and New Testaments: "In the past God spoke to our forefathers through the prophets at many times and in various ways, but in these last days he has spoken to us by his Son, whom he appointed heir of all things, and through whom he made the universe" (Hebrews 1:1-2 NIV). He goes on to clarify both the significance of the biblical writings and the process through which they came to us: "We must pay more careful attention, therefore, to what we have heard, so that we do not drift away. For if the message spoken by angels was binding, and every violation and disobedience received its just punishment, how shall we escape if we ignore such a great salvation? This salvation, which was first announced by the Lord, was confirmed to us by those who heard him. God also testified to it by signs, wonders and various miracles, and gifts of the Holy Spirit distributed according to his will" (Hebrews 2:1-4 NIV).

God used dreams, visions, burning bushes, direct and audible communication, and more to relay his message through his prophets. This message was recorded in what we call the Old Testament. The principal message of the Old Testament found its fulfillment in the person of Jesus Christ, the final, ultimate revelation of God. Jesus then communicated to his apostles in both word and deed. This communication was preserved and recorded for us in the New Testament. Thus, in the Bible we have access to God's self-revelation to man.

This is not to say that the Bible is the only place one can find truth. God, for example, has revealed himself in nature. The psalmist says, "Nature declares the glory of God." Moreover, Romans clearly states: "For since the creation of the world His invisible attributes, His eternal power and divine nature, have been clearly seen, being understood through what has been made, so that they are without excuse" (Romans 1:20).

Many writings and/or teachings contain truth to some degree. The Bible is set apart, however, in that it does not merely contain truth; it *is* truth—complete truth without any mixture of error.

As I said earlier, I like to play the role of amateur chef. I am so taken with cooking that on holidays, my wife and children (and my mother, my brother-in-law, my cousins—you get the point) buy me cooking utensils or recipe books instead of ties (glory to God!). I enjoy mastering a recipe and making it for guests. One of my big hits is a homemade barbeque sauce. I'm not talking about the kind where you mix up your favorite brands of sauce and add some "secret ingredients;" I'm talkin' about my kitchen cookin', my season-and-spice addin', my overnight-Crock-Pot-soakin' homemade, my from-the-ground-up, Egyptian Mummy Bar-B-Que Sauce! By the way, I call it "Egyptian Mummy" because when you make it just right you don't need an alarm clock to wake you up the next morning. It will call you out of your sleep and wake you up like one of those mummies in a horror film.

On one occasion, though, my sauce was nothing to brag about. We had just moved to a new house, and I could not find my recipe. I had just begun making the sauce, but I thought I had mastered it to the degree that I could make it from memory. Boy, was I wrong! It was awful. It was so bad, I didn't even offer it to my family. I just threw it out. Thankfully, because we were in a new neighborhood, the neighbors had not yet discovered my sauce. Otherwise things could have gotten ugly as I tried to explain to an angry mob why they could not partake of the delectable delight they have now come to love. Eventually, I found my recipe and discovered my mistakes. There were only a couple of difficulties, but they were enough to destroy the sauce.

God's truth is like that. All of us crave truth. In fact, we were designed to crave it. We also know what it tastes like. That's why a half-truth is far worse than a whole lie. Some people—and some religions—have discovered part of God's truth, but it has been mixed with lies. They may admit that God exists and that he is the Creator, but they add to these good and essential ingredients a mixture of legalism and distorted Christology, hence corrupting the entire recipe. In the Bible, however, we have the pure, unadulterated truth. And when we come to it, we can "taste and see that the LORD is good" (Psalm 34:8).

Ultimately, a human could not have produced the Bible alone. Anyone who has read the Scriptures carefully and with an open mind would see God's fingerprints all over the text. The authority, the majesty, the splendor, the prophecy and the overall approach to sin and holiness simply transcend humanity.

The way I see it, there are three possible sources of the Bible. First, some kind of evil spirit (i.e., the devil) could have given us the Bible in order to deceive us. This possibility, however, does not make sense. Why would an evil spirit give us a text that first makes itself the adversary and ultimately teaches us how to overcome evil? Second, the Bible could be the exclusive work of men. This possibility raises a related question: What kind of persons would have written the Bible? If evil men wrote the Bible, they fall into the aforementioned category of something that is illogical. They have written a text that brings them nothing but condemnation. On the other hand, if good men wrote the Bible, they have made claims about God that are not true, which makes them not good men but evil men. The third and final possibility is that the Bible could have come from God *through* men. This is the only solution without internal moral conflict.

9
THE JESUS
OF THE BIBLE

In the essentials, unity; in the nonessentials, liberty; in all things, charity," runs a maxim often attributed to Augustine of Hippo. What, then, are the essentials? What are those doctrinal issues surrounding the person and work of Jesus on which we must agree? Moreover, what is the source of these truths?

One of my first real jobs was in a group home. I was twenty-one, a senior in college. I worked in a house full of teenage boys. Their problems ranged from abandonment to abuse, to drug use and behavioral problems. They were black, white, Hispanic—you name it. However, they all had one thing in common: they were all fatherless. Some had been abused or abandoned by their fathers; others had never met the men whom they referred to as "my old man." However, that never kept many of them from telling elaborate stories about their dads.

I can't tell you how many of these kids' fathers were professional athletes, businessmen, big-time gangsters, or just millionaires—at least, according to their sons. The stories were as numerous as they were astonishing. "My old man played college ball." "Oh yeah? My old man played in the pros!" "So what, my old man has a Super Bowl ring." On and on the stories would go. Each story was more extravagant than the next, and none of them were true.

It was as though the boys didn't know that the staff had access to their files and that we knew that their fathers were convicts, addicts, child molesters, or worse. Or maybe they just didn't care. Maybe the myth was more comforting than the truth. These myths were so strong that not even a visit from one of the boys' fathers could shake them.

We can understand why boys like these need to employ myths as coping mechanisms, yet we can agree that these mechanisms do not alter reality. The boys' fathers did not become what they envisioned or invented; they simply were who and what they had always been. The same can be said about Jesus.

Many people wish to recreate Jesus in an image befitting their presuppositions, but that simply will not do. Jesus is who he always has been. Jesus does not morph into the image that we suggest. He simply is! Thus, the question with which we must wrestle is not "What do most people think?" but rather, "What do the facts say?" And since our most reliable source of information about the person, nature, and work of Jesus is the Bible, the more precise question is, "What does the text say?"

It is impossible to exhaust all of the information in the Bible about the person and work of Jesus. Therefore, we must find a manageable yet comprehensive body of information with which we may equip ourselves to present a concise, biblical, and comprehensive argument. Perhaps the most concise, yet comprehensive presentation of the person and work of Jesus is found in the New Testament preaching on salvation through Christ that is known as the *kerygma* (or "core content of the gospel"). While the kerygma was not formalized in the New Testament, its presence is unmistakable. The content consists of five basic points:

1. Jesus is God, as attested to by his miracles.
2. God became a man (born of a virgin).
3. As a man Jesus suffered and died for sin (substitution-ary atonement).
4. Jesus was resurrected from the dead and ascended into heaven.
5. Jesus is coming again.

The most comprehensive presentations of the kerygma occur in Philippians 2 and Acts 2. In the first instance Paul uses the kerygma as a model for Christian attitudes. In the Acts passage, Peter is preaching on the day of Pentecost and is directing his comments toward a non-Christian audience. In both cases, though, the person and work of Jesus is outlined clearly. Both apostles demonstrate that knowing these five key components is essential both for coming to know Christ and for following him. Hence, they form the ideal foundation for reintroducing Jesus to our culture.

In defending these key assertions, we must keep three important points in mind. First, we must use the Bible in context. It is important that we do more than just snatch portions of verses out of the passages in which they appear. We must be true to the text, and we must present arguments that will not fall apart upon further scrutiny. Second, we must demonstrate that each of these ideas is presented throughout the Scriptures. We should not build entire doctrines on singular statements. Third, we should keep conflicting views in mind in order to anticipate and answer objections. With that in mind, let's look more closely at each of the five components of the kerygma.

Jesus is God.

The evidence for the divinity of Christ is found throughout the New Testament, but for our purposes we will concentrate on three key passages: John 1, Colossians 1, and 1 John 1. The reasons for choosing these texts are twofold. First, because they are all found in the first chapter of the book in which they appear, they are easier to remember. Second, these are chunks of Scripture that present the idea in context as opposed to single verses that may support these ideas but carry less weight by themselves.

Because the Bible is a consistent compilation, there will be overlap between these key passages. However, I will walk you through each passage and point out the key themes to be explained during presentations. First, let us examine John 1:1–5: "In the beginning was the Word, and the Word was with God, and the Word was God. He was in the beginning with God. All things came into being through Him, and apart from Him nothing came into being that has come into being. In Him was life, and the life was the Light of men. The Light shines in the darkness, but the darkness did not comprehend it."

While there are many things that can be said about this passage, the key is to understand and be able to present the major themes. Also, since our idea is to present these points to people who are not familiar with Jesus, we must keep it simple and make observations that they will be able to follow. In other words, discussions about definite articles in verse 1 should be reserved for another time. (If you don't understand what I mean, you should definitely see my point about keeping things simple!)

One important element to consider when dealing with John 1 is that "the Word" is a reference to Jesus, but this fact doesn't become clear until verse 14. Therefore, take your time and explain that before you get to the statements about Christ's divinity.

Jesus is eternal.

Verse 1 opens with the familiar declaration, "In the beginning was the Word." This text fits with Genesis 1:1, "In the beginning God." John uses the Greek equivalent of the Hebrew phrase employed by Moses in Genesis 1:1 in order to make a point about the eternal existence of Jesus. This phrase hearkens to a time before time, a place before the world, and a person before humankind. This phrase points to a time when all there was, was God. This phrase points back to eternity.

Micah 5:2 makes clear that the Messiah who would be born in Bethlehem was one whose "origins are from of old, from ancient times." Isaiah prophesied that the child who would be given to us would be both "Mighty God" and "Everlasting Father" (Isaiah 9:6). In fact Jesus himself made reference to his eternity when he stated, "I tell you the truth, . . . before Abraham was born, I am" (John 8:58). Jesus is eternal! There was never a moment when he wasn't, and there will never be a moment when he is not.

Jesus shares the Father's nature and essence.

Jesus is not like God; he is not close to God; he *is* God! Jesus shares the Father's nature; he is of the same substance. Paul echoes this fact in Philippians 2:6 when he states that "although He existed in the form of God, [Jesus] did not did not regard equality with God a thing to be grasped" (NIV). This is a statement of both the preexistence of Christ and of his eternal divinity.

At least four vital factors of this doctrine must be preserved: Jesus' divinity, his humanity, the complete preservation of his two natures, and the lack of conflict between the two. Stated another way, Jesus as his incarnation was fully man and fully God. and there was no conflict between those natures.

Jesus is distinct from the Father.

This is one of the most difficult truths to communicate, yet we must not overlook it. The text makes a clear distinction between the Father and Jesus; they are distinct persons. Jesus is not just the Father in the flesh. As we shall see, the Father and

Son (and the Spirit) share the same nature and essence, but they are revealed to us as distinct persons who exist in relation to each other.

The distinctions are borne out in two events, when Jesus prays to the Father and when the Father communicates his affirmation of Jesus at his baptism. Even though the Trinity is difficult to explain, it is essential truth and should not be avoided.

Jesus is the Creator of everything.

John declares, "Through him all things were made; without him nothing was made that has been made" (NIV). What a clear, succinct, powerful proclamation! Jesus is the Creator of the world. Paul echoes this statement in Colossians 1:16 when he writes, "For by him all things were created: things in heaven and on earth, visible and invisible, whether thrones or powers or rulers or authorities; all things were created by him and for him" (NIV).

Creation is the prerogative of deity. Jesus cannot be the Creator of the universe without being God. Note also that both writers attribute the creation of *all* things to Jesus. Thus, it should not be assumed that he was the first creation. This flies in the face of the clear intent of the text.

Jesus forgave sins.

In Mark 2, we find Jesus healing the paralytic. However, there is much more involved here than just healing. The furor over these events was not caused by the fact that a man's companions had to drop him through a hole in the roof in order to get him to Jesus, nor was it due to the fact that a man who had been paralyzed when he arrived carried his own pallet away when he left. No, the furor was over the fact that Jesus forgave the man's sins.

Jesus exposes the conundrum in verses 8–11: "Immediately Jesus knew in his spirit that this was what they were thinking in their hearts, and he said to them, 'Why are you thinking these things? Which is easier: to say to the paralytic, "Your sins are forgiven," or to say, "Get up, take your mat and walk"? But that you may know that the Son of Man has authority on earth to forgive sins. . . .' He said to the paralytic, 'I tell you, get up, take your mat and go home'" (NIV).

Clearly, those present understood that a man could forgive another for a wrong done to him, but no ordinary man had the authority to forgive sins in this way. Here we see a clear indication that Jesus is God.

God became a man, being born to a virgin.

A college student once looked me in the eye, saying, "If God really wants people to believe he is real, why doesn't he just show himself?" I couldn't help but smile as I realized that in an effort to stump me, he had stumbled upon one of the most crucial elements of the gospel message: God became a man. This young man was absolutely correct. It makes complete sense that God would reveal himself personally to mankind, and that is precisely what he did in the incarnation: "In the sixth month the angel Gabriel was sent to the city of Galilee called Nazareth to a virgin engaged to a man whose name was Joseph, of the descendants of David; and the virgin's name was Mary" (Luke 1:26–27).

Luke gives an account of events that came before what is arguably the greatest of all miracles, the Incarnation of Jesus. Some would argue that the Resurrection would have to be considered the greatest miracle, and perhaps that is true. But don't forget that the Incarnation makes the Resurrection possible. We could have had the Resurrection without water being turned into wine or withered hands being made whole. However, the Incarnation stands as the only other *essential* miracle. God became a man as a prerequisite to his atoning death and resurrection. In any case, the Incarnation cannot be overemphasized.

There are several key points that we must emphasize when sharing the truth of the incarnation. First, the fact is that God became a man; it was not the other way around. Mormons, for example, believe that a man (*Elohim*) became a god. Furthermore, they teach that we, too, can become gods and inherit our own planets to rule. This is not the message of the Bible. Nor is it compatible in any way with Christianity. We have already established that Jesus is eternal. Thus, the idea that he inherited divinity is ludicrous.

Second, it is important to note that the physical conception of Jesus was a moment of incarnation, not a moment of creation. Jesus did not come into being in Mary's womb; he merely clothed himself in flesh. Eternal God became a baby in a young girl's womb. Paul paints this picture beautifully in Philippians 2:5–7 when he writes, "Your attitude should be the same as that of Christ Jesus: Who, being in very nature God, did not consider equality with God something to be grasped, but made himself nothing, taking the very nature of a servant, being made in human likeness" (NIV).

Third, it is important to note that the virgin birth is different from the Catholic doctrine of immaculate conception. The doctrine of Immaculate Conception contends that Mary was sinless and remained a perpetual virgin. This argument has no basis in Scripture and is in fact directly refuted by the Bible. For example, the Bible makes clear reference to Jesus' brothers and sisters (of course they would have been half brothers and sisters), one of whom was the apostle James. This doctrine is dangerous in that it ascribes sinlessness and ultimately a mediatory role to someone other than Christ. Both claims directly contradict the clear teaching of Scripture (Romans 3:10, 23; 1 Timothy 2:5).

As a man, Jesus suffered and died for sin (substitutionary atonement).

Every other religion in the world suggests that we must have some sort of religious experience and from that point on do more good things than bad in order to gain entrance into Paradise. Perhaps that is why the most common answers to the question, "Why do you believe you are going to heaven when you die?" all begin with something to the effect of, "I am basically a good person," or "I treat other people the way I want to be treated," or "I never harm anyone else." In short, all of these claims arise out of the same philosophical foundation. God watches what we do and records our deeds in order to keep score for the end. These assumptions are contrary to the message of the Bible.

Man is sinful.

In Romans 3:23, Paul writes, "For all have sinned and fall short of the glory of God." The literal meaning for the word translated "sin" is "missing the mark." Sinning involves both actions and attitudes that fail to measure up to God's standard of righteousness. Another verse captures this idea: "All of us like sheep have gone astray, each of us has turned to his own way" (Isaiah 53:6). Again, we see the emphasis on our gravitation away from the righteous standard of God.

Many people believe that humankind is basically good and that one's environment causes one to sin. I am convinced that those people don't have kids! Anyone who has children knows that we have to teach them everything . . . except how to sin. They come here with that knowledge.

The most popular illustration of sin is the story of the archer and the arrow. It is commonly said that sin is like shooting an arrow and missing the bull's-eye. This illustration paints a poignant picture, but it misses a key element of sin. It is not as though we are walking through life taking aim at righteousness and missing. In the overwhelming majority of cases, we aren't even taking a shot.

Another way of looking at sin is to see God's righteousness as a piece of music sitting on a piano in the middle of a house. This is not just any piece of music; this piece is the righteousness of God, and only those who play it to perfection will be in right relationship with him. By the way, the music is not just complicated—it's impossible.

In that house are people who walk by the piano as though it were not there. Others occasionally sit down and tap on the keys. Still others skillfully play music of their own design. Still others find God's piece and attempt to play it to the best of their ability. In any case, both the players and the nonplayers, both those who play their own music and those who play God's music inaccurately have "missed the mark."

You see, sin is not limited to those who aim at God's righteousness and miss; it also involves those who choose to ignore God's righteousness and never take a shot. The people who know and follow the Word of God to the best of their ability are sinners. The people in this world who have made lists of things they must do, or not do, in order to be righteous and who fail to follow through on the lists are sinners. Those people who develop their own religions and philosophies to which they adhere as best they can are sinners. And those people who wander aimlessly through life doing what feels right at the moment are sinners. We are all sinners!

God is holy and just, and he must punish sin.

Just as light, by its very nature, repels darkness, God by his very nature repels sin. God is holy. This does not mean that God is just *really* good. It literally means that God is "other." He is set apart. God is not like man since God shares none of the human's flaws or shortcomings. God is inherently different from sinful man. There is nothing in God that is compatible with sin. Hence, sin finds no favor with God and is always utterly repelled by him.

If you have ever tried to push two magnets together, you have seen a physical picture of this spiritual reality. No matter how hard you push, those two magnets seem to fight tooth-and-nail to stay apart. If they are to attract, the charge will have to be changed in one of them. It is the same with God. His character does not allow sin to approach. The only way for sinners to approach is for them to be changed.

Sinners cannot satisfy the righteous requirements of God.

Ask the average person if he or she is a Christian, and you will more than likely get an answer like, "Of course I am," or "I think so." Venture a little deeper into their answers, however, and you will discover that most people who think they are Christians are, in fact, not. I cannot tell you how many times I have started a conversation with people who told me they were Christians and ended up leading them to faith in Christ. Almost always, their confusion involves this issue of works versus grace; they simply do not know that sinners cannot satisfy the righteous requirements of God. This fact is evident by their answers to a simple question, "Why do you say you are a Christian?" Here are a few of the wrong answers to that question.

1. "Of course I am a Christian; I go to church every Sunday." One of the most common misconceptions among people in our highly churched culture is that going to church on Sundays is somehow enough to satisfy the righteous requirements of God. People who believe that way really ought to be afraid to spend time in their garage because if you believe that going to church every Sunday will make you a Christian, the same logic would say that going to your garage every day will eventually make you a car.

Of course, the analogy is not quite that simple, but you get the point. There are plenty of people who go to church every week and have absolutely nothing to show for it, just as there are people who spend several years in college and never seem to move toward graduation. While consistency and patience are good qualities, something more is involved.

2. "I was raised in a Christian home." I must admit that the first time I heard this one it saddened me. Keep in mind, I hadn't grown up in church and thus was not exposed to "Christian lingo." The first time someone said to me that they were Christian because they had grown up in a Christian home, I believe I said something like, "Oh, I'm sorry. Did your parents die? Is that why you were sent to a 'Christian home'?" I could not fathom the idea of a person who belonged to Jesus blaming it on his or her family tree! However, there are those who actually believe that because their mother, father, and grandparents were Christian, they are automatically Christians themselves.

3. "I've been a Christian all my life." This one saddens me. I often meet people who come from religious backgrounds that expose them to childhood rituals like infant baptism. Unfortunately, many of these people believe that those childhood rituals are a substitute for a personal, intimate relationship with God through his Son Jesus Christ. They believe that these rituals somehow circumvent the act of hearing the gospel and responding to it, when in fact, nothing could be further from the truth.

I meet young people regularly who are struggling with their salvation because of this very issue. "I was baptized when I was very young," they often confess, "and I did not understand what I was doing." Or worse yet, some admit that they experienced some ritual as an infant and thought they were in right relationship with God because of it. Inevitably, this leads to a crisis of faith.

4. "I *think* I am a Christian." This is another dead giveaway. Whenever I hear someone say they "think" they are Christian, I simply begin to share the gospel. I don't believe a person can truly belong to God and not know it. As far as I'm concerned, that's like a person being married and not knowing it. The fact is that coming to Christ is a volitional act of the will. It is an exercise of faith. It is not an accident.

This is not the same as a Christian who has doubts. I have met several people who fell into practices that they had thought were in their past and who consequently thought that perhaps they were never really saved. That kind of doubt is different. Those kinds of doubts come. What I am talking about is a person who does not really know how to become a Christian or what it means to be one, and thus says, "I *think* I am a Christian." This person is lost.

5. "Yes, I'm a Christian. I was born right here in the United States." Don't laugh! I have actually heard this one on several occasions. Worse yet, I had one gentleman tell me, "Of course I'm a Christian. I was born in Texas." While I am as proud to be a Texan as the next guy (usually more), I must confess that this one threw me. At the root of this perspective is the logic that says, "America is a Christian nation. I am an American. Therefore, I must be a Christian."

While all of these beliefs have their own unique problems, they all arise from the same presupposition—that salvation is earned. We believe that by going to church or being raised by Christians, or being good, or being Texans, we can somehow satisfy God and earn salvation. There are at least three major problems with this type of thinking: It ignores the clear teaching of Scripture; it ignores the nature of man; and it nullifies the work of Christ.

The Bible could not be clearer about our ability to earn salvation. One of the most explicit statements of this truth is found in Paul's words from Romans 3:21–24: "But now a righteousness from God, apart from law, has been made known, to which the Law and the Prophets testify. This righteousness from God comes through faith in Jesus Christ to all who believe. There is no difference, for all have sinned and fall short of the glory of God, and are justified freely by his grace through the redemption that came by Christ Jesus" (NIV).

The Bible leaves no room for persons to be good enough to earn God's favor. This argument is fortified in many other passages, such as Psalms 14:1–3 and 53:1–3, Romans 3:10, Ephesians 1:7 and 2:8, and James 2:10.

We also see in this statement that we by our very nature are incapable of achieving the type of righteousness God requires. Paul refers to this type of righteousness as "the righteousness of God" and clearly distinguishes it from anything that can be achieved by the Law. You and I will never be "good enough." God's standard does not allow for a margin of error. Besides, if any one of us is good enough, the work of Christ was in vain. Paul continues: "Whom God displayed publicly as a propitiation in His blood through faith. This was to demonstrate His righteousness, because in the forbearance of God He passed over the sins previously committed; for the demonstration, I say, of His righteousness at the present time, that He would be just and justifier of the one who has faith in Jesus" (Romans 3:25–26).

The word *propitiation* means that Jesus satisfied the righteous requirement of God. Going back to the music illustration, we could say that Jesus came into the room, sat down at the piano and played to perfection the piece God had given. What that illustration does not capture, however, is the gruesome fact that the "piece of music" God required was a sinless, sacrificial, substitutionary death. Listen to both the logic and eloquence of Paul's summation: "Where then is boasting? It is excluded. By what kind of law? Of works? No, but by a law of faith. For we maintain that a man is justified by faith apart from works of the Law" (Romans 3:27–28).

We get no credit! Neither you nor I can lay claim to any part of our salvation. We have absolutely no reason to boast. A similar statement is found in Ephesians 2:8–9: "For it is by grace you have been saved through faith; and that not of yourselves, it is the gift of God; not as a result of works, so that no one may boast."

I don't know if you caught this, but not even the faith we use to trust Christ is ours. God is sovereign over our salvation from beginning to end. It was this fact that led Martin Luther to proclaim, "*Sola Dei Gloria,*" or as I like to paraphrase it, all glory and honor be to our God!

If Christianity is to thrive in our post-Christian culture, we must articulate clearly the doctrine of salvation by grace. Imagine how many people cross our paths with a faulty understanding of this doctrine. I believe this is one of Satan's greatest deceptions. What better way to keep people from heaven than to convince them that they are saved when they are not? However, we need not fear. As I said earlier, our God is sovereign, and he will prevail. I just want to make sure I am answering the bell and doing my part.

Jesus was our substitute and atonement for sin.

Here is the dilemma: God created man and woman with the intent of entering into relationship with them. However, through the actions of one man, Adam, sin entered the world and mankind fell. Hence, due to his holiness, righteousness, and justice, God had no choice but to destroy sin (and sinners). Therefore, man's sin alienated him from God. The only answer to this dilemma lay in the person of Jesus Christ. Jesus was the only means by which the righteous requirements of God could be met, through Christ's sinless life, without the total destruction of all humankind. Peter said it best when he wrote, "For Christ also died for sins once for all, the just for the unjust, so that He might bring us to God" (1 Peter 3:18).

Jesus rose from the dead (resurrection) and ascended into heaven.

The Resurrection has been referred to as the "capstone in the arch of Christianity." The importance of this doctrine cannot be overstated. Without the resurrection, there is no promise of eternal life. Without the resurrection, there is no validation of the earthly ministry and/or teaching of Jesus. Without the Resurrection there is no authentic Christianity. As Paul argues, without the resurrection, we are of all men "most pitiable" (1 Corinthians 15:19 NKJV).

Nonetheless, in this age of religious relativism, tolerance, and philosophical pluralism, there are those who claim to hold to a form of Christianity that denies this essential doctrine. John Dominic Crossan, one of the leaders of the Jesus Seminar, for example, when interviewed by Peter Jennings for his special, *The Search for Jesus*, made these comments: "The purpose of crucifixion was state terrorism and the function was to leave the body on the cross for the carrion crows and the prowling dogs. It was not simply that it made you suffer a lot—it meant you didn't get buried. That's what made it one of the supreme Roman penalties: lack of burial. As I read those stories, I feel terribly sympathetic for the followers of Jesus because I hear hope there; not history."

Crossan chooses to ignore the fact that Jesus was crucified just prior to a high holy day and thus would not have been allowed to linger on the cross. Here we have a prime example of the lengths to which some people will go to redefine Jesus. Historically, there are several classic attempts to deny the Resurrection.

The Swoon Theory

For centuries people have made attempts to explain away Jesus' resurrection. According to the swoon theory, Jesus did not actually die on the cross; he just "swooned." Thinking he was dead, the soldiers took him down, saw to his burial, and guarded his tomb, all the while unaware of the fact that he was still alive. The swoon theory argues that the resurrected Christ was not resurrected at all, because he had not died.

There are myriad problems with this theory. First, it ignores the gruesome facts surrounding the crucifixion of Jesus. Jesus was whipped with a cat-o'-nine-tails, beaten beyond recognition, dragged through town, pierced in his hands and feet, hung on a cross, stabbed in the heart, wrapped from head to toe, placed in a dark, damp tomb, and all of this after a night of sweating drops of blood (a condition which would have exacerbated the effects of each of the previous actions). Yet he did not die!

Second, the swoon theory requires monumental blunders by numerous trained executioners. The men who oversaw the crucifixion of Jesus were professional soldiers who would have been trained in the deadly art of crucifixion. They knew how to kill a man, and they knew when a man was dead. This was the purpose of the spear thrust in Jesus' side. They would not have taken Jesus off the cross had he not been dead. They would have broken his legs in order to hasten death and then put him in a tomb.

Third, this theory requires a *Mission Impossible* escape from the tomb. Think about it: Jesus is in the tomb, near death; then, all of a sudden, he shakes himself awake, wiggles out of the wrappings, folds them up neatly, and places them in the corner, single-handedly moves a boulder weighing several tons, performs some kind of magic spell on the guards so they don't wake up, and limps away to the predetermined meeting place. Get serious! It takes more faith to believe this than it does to believe that he rose from the dead.

Fourth, according to this theory, a man beaten beyond recognition who lost enough blood to fill a blood bank was able to convince a dozen (minus one) cowards that his current physical state represented victory over death. Imagine the look on the disciples' faces when Jesus gave them the Great Commission, declaring that "all authority has been given to Me in heaven and on earth" (Matthew 28:18), while someone held him up to keep him from falling from the effects of blood loss.

In short, the swoon theory is an implausible attempt to explain away the Resurrection.

The Conspiracy Theory

According to the conspiracy theory, the crucifixion happened just as the Bible says it did (sort of), but after the burial, the disciples decided to make up a lie. They would tell people that Jesus rose from the dead just like he had predicted. Marvin Meyer explained it this way on Peter Jennings' special: "One of the greatest difficulties that early Christians had if they were going to cope with the reality of the crucifixion of Jesus is what do you do with that? How do you keep the movement going? How do you have some hope in the face of this kind of shameful and horrible death? And one of the things I believe that early Christians did, is they took the model of the mystery religions. They took that story and retold that story as the story of Jesus."

Meyer makes three assertions: First, the goal of the conspiracy was to "keep the movement going." In other words, they knew that their leader had lied, but they wanted to continue to attract crowds. Next, the crucifixion of Jesus (though he himself had predicted it) was "shameful and horrible." Why? Because Meyer is suggesting that the crucifixion was not followed by a resurrection! Finally, the disciples either maliciously or out of desperation latched onto a Greek myth and simply portrayed Jesus as a mythological superhero. In other words, all those things Jesus said about being crucified and resurrected were not only untrue; he never even said them. They were merely added after his death in order to hide the shame of his failure.

The conspiracy theory is based upon a few crucial presuppositions. First, there is the question of the dead man in the tomb. That's right. If the disciples made up the whole story, they would first have to steal the body. In that case, we would have another *Mission Impossible* episode with those sniveling cowards sneaking in under cover of darkness, removing the stone, and stealing the body without alerting the guards.

Second, this theory does not explain the sudden transformation of the disciples from a group of scared men, huddled in the upper room, to a band of brothers preaching the gospel to every creature with whom they came in contact. Remember, all of these men, with the exception of John and Peter, were nowhere to be found during the crucifixion. In fact, Peter, when confronted by, among others, a little girl, began to swear and call down curses in an effort to distance himself from Jesus, not just once but three times. During the days that followed, they were all gathered together in the upper room "for fear of the Jews" (John 20:19). This does not sound like a group of men who would conspire to tell a tale that would eventually cost them their lives.

The third and most difficult question for the conspiracy theory to answer is the question of martyrdom. Are we really supposed to believe that these men died the most gruesome deaths imaginable for a lie that they had concocted?

The Hallucination Theory

Perhaps the most amusing theory is the hallucination theory. The disciples merely thought they saw the resurrected Christ, but in fact, they were hallucinating. That's right, it was all in their minds. Jesus never rose from the dead; they just imagined the whole thing. Most scholars attempt to state this theory tactfully. For instance, Paula Fredriksen, another guest on Peter Jennings's special, stated it this way: "I know in their own terms what they saw was the raised Jesus. That's what they say and then all the historic evidence we have afterwards attests to their conviction that that's what they saw. I'm not saying that they really did see the raised Jesus. I wasn't there. I don't know what they saw, but I do know, as a historian, that they must have seen something."

Note that Fredriksen says the historic evidence attests to the disciples' "conviction," not to the facts. In other words, there is no doubt that they believed what they said. However, according to those who hold to the hallucination theory, what they saw was not real.

First, we have the dead man in the tomb—again. In this case, there would have been no stolen body; the body would still have been in the tomb. In this case, anyone who wished to disprove the message being preached after the hallucination would merely have to go to the tomb and view the body.

Second, these hallucinations happened in successive meetings on multiple occasions and in multiple locations. First, the women came to the tomb to anoint Jesus' body, and they hallucinated. They went to get Peter and John, and the disciples joined in the hallucination. Peter and John went back to the upper room, where all of the disciples hallucinated together. Thomas, however, missed out on the hallucination, so they did it all over again when he arrived. After this the men on the road to Emmaus hallucinated separately, and eventually five hundred brethren hallucinated at one time. That is some kind of hallucination!

All of these theories stretch the limits of credulity. In fact, I find it hard to believe that there have been, and still are, people who accept these theories rather than believe the message of the Gospels. Every one of these concepts is born out of a desire to explain Christianity in nonsupernatural terms. If the Resurrection never happened, then Christianity is just like any other religion. We have a teacher who was a good man and a good prophet and brought to light some incredible truths but no more. He is no different from any other great man who taught great truths. If the resurrection is real, however, Jesus is so much more than just another teacher. He is God!

Jesus will return (second coming).

Perhaps the most difficult point of the kerygma to accept is the final point, that Jesus is coming again. It is especially difficult for those of us who live some two thousand years on the other side of his Crucifixion and Resurrection. It had to be easier when he had just been resurrected two years ago, or even twenty years ago. Now we look back over two millennia and sometimes wonder, when? To make matters worse, skeptics will use belief in the Second Coming like a club.

Countless self-proclaimed experts have given us timetables and scenarios that have failed time and time again. Who can forget the book *88 Reasons Jesus Will Return in 1988*? Some groups have chosen to redefine the Second Coming, opting instead for a belief in a "spiritual" as opposed to a bodily return of Christ when their timetables fail. However, the Bible seems to suggest another way. Don't predict. Simply believe and proclaim.

10
NOT THE WHAT
BUT THE HOW

"Sometimes it's not what we say; it's how we say it!" How many times have we heard that one? Or how about this one: "They don't care how much you know till they know how much you care." I guess the reason we have heard these maxims so much is that they're true. It is great to memorize Scriptures and answers to potential objections, but all of our hard work is moot if our attitudes undermine our presentations. The key to winning people is being a winsome person with a worthwhile message. We know we have a worthwhile message. In fact, it is the greatest message ever known. The question remains: Are we winsome people?

These truths are only heightened by the current philosophical climate. Christians are presumed to be intolerant, narrow-minded, Bible-thumping bigots. Hence, we often get only one shot when it comes to presenting the gospel. If we prove to be exactly what people expect, we may miss our opportunity. However, if we shatter the stereotypes with a winsome approach, we just may get our foot in the door. This is what I like to call "earning the right to share."

I do not mean to imply that Christians must "earn" free speech. Nor do I mean that we must prove our worth. The simple fact, though, is that people's presuppositions serve as walls over which truth is sometimes not allowed to climb. The way we choose to treat people can often lower those walls. I learned this lesson during a week of evangelism at Stanford and San Jose State Universities in northern California.

It was a beautiful spring day. I remember looking out of the window at the rolling hills as we drove from Palo Alto to San Jose. For a brief moment, I actually missed living in the Golden State. We had finished our work for the day at Stanford and were on our way to SJSU to do some open-air preaching and personal witnessing.

When we arrived, the campus was abuzz with activity. Students zipped by on bikes and rollerblades as they made their way to and from their late-morning classes. We checked in with the administration, found our assigned space in the quad (the center of campus activity), and set up our base of operations. Christian students from both campuses were scheduled to meet in our staging area during the busiest time of the day. Once gathered, we would begin an impromptu worship service comprised of a song and a brief sermon.

As I began to preach about the importance of having direction in life, students began to gather from every corner of the campus. Some came to listen, others just to see what the crowd was about. Still others came to get involved by shouting in opposition. It was pure chaos, and I loved every minute of it. After a few moments, I ended my comments, and the students fanned out to engage the remaining congregators.

In the midst of the crowd, I saw a young woman walking toward me. Her face was set and stern, and her gait was filled with purpose. As she got closer, I noticed her clothes. She had on a pair of faded blue jeans, a white T-shirt, a pair of combat boots, and an old army jacket. She looked like a member of a radical paramilitary group. Her hair was short and shaved on the sides, and she wore no makeup or jewelry.

She identified herself as a member of a group organized to defend gay rights and advance the cause of gay and lesbian students on the campus. I could tell by her demeanor that she was not interested in polite discussion. She stood as close to me as she could and stared me directly in my eyes as if to challenge me physically. As I stated earlier, I am not a small man. Moreover, she was not a large woman. Nevertheless, it was obvious that she wanted any kind of confrontation that she could get.

I knew immediately that she was attempting to demonstrate to the watching crowd that we were a bunch of hate-filled, homophobic bigots. I immediately asked God for wisdom, and he answered. I never raised my voice, though she practically shouted as she asked me, "Are you telling me that I am going to go to hell?" I responded by presenting the gospel in affirmative statements. Instead of, "Yes, you are going to hell if you don't receive Jesus," I responded, "All we are saying is that all people have a sin problem and that Jesus has provided the only answer."

She began to appear frustrated by the fact that I would not engage in a shouting match. Eventually she agreed to take one of the tracts we were handing out and went away. After a while, the crowd died down. We were about to gather our things and leave when, out of the corner of my eye, I saw the same young woman approaching again. This time her countenance was different. She had actually read the tract and had some legitimate questions. I answered her questions, and she merely nodded her head.

As the conversation ended, I had an overwhelming urge to pray for this young woman. At first, I just thought the Lord wanted me to remember her in prayer after we were gone. Then I realized that the moment was now! I looked at her and asked, "Would it be all right if I said a prayer for you?" There was what seemed to be an inordinately long pause as the students who were gathering up our things stopped and awaited the young lady's answer. What would she say? Would she become irate and start yelling again? Would she throw the tract in my face? Would she bombard me with profanity as she had done earlier? Or would she say yes?

Much to my amazement, she slowly raised her head, looked into my eyes and asked, "Would you really do that for me?" Her voice quivered as she realized that I was serious. I smiled at her and said, "I would be honored to pray for you right now." She didn't quite know what to do so she sheepishly lowered her head and closed her eyes.

I placed my hand on her shoulder and began to pray for her. As I began to pray, she started to shake. It was as though no one had ever touched her without an ulterior motive. Soon tears began to stream down her cheeks as I asked God to reveal himself to her and show her how much he loved her. I don't remember that young lady's name, but I will never forget the way her entire countenance transformed during that two-minute prayer. It was as though an unseen river of grace flowed down the middle of that campus and drenched her from head to toe.

As the prayer ended, she thanked me without giving any eye contact, then hurried away as if she were trying to avoid anyone seeing her emotions. I never saw her again. I do not know what happened to her. I don't know if she took that tract and prayed to receive Christ or regrouped and explained away everything that happened in order to continue in her lifestyle. I do know, however, that God used her to teach me a very important lesson about sharing Christ with people: Sometimes it is not the *what*, but the *how* that makes the difference.

There is no magic formula for showing people that we care, but there are some things that we can keep in mind as we share. These are things that are bound to impact both those to whom the Lord allows us to speak and those of us who share.

Don't forget your sin.

It is important to remember that the Lord saves sinners. I know this sounds simplistic, but I am often surprised at how easy it is for believers to forget that we, too, need a Savior. Some of us act like we are going to heaven on our own merit as opposed to counting on the imputed righteousness of Christ.

The fact is that it would have taken no more grace to save that radical lesbian activist than it did to save me! "All have sinned and fall short of the glory of God" (Romans 3:23). It is essential to remember that there was a time when we did not know that we were walking in sin and someone had to point the way to Jesus in order for us to be redeemed.

Don't forget your Savior.

One of my favorite Bible stories is that of the woman at the well in John 4. I love the ways Jesus shattered convention and tradition in order to demonstrate the power and breadth and depth of his grace. First, one would not have expected Rabbi Jesus to be seen with a woman. There were strict customs that would have made such a meeting taboo. Second, this was a woman with a reputation who had been married five times and was currently shacking up with a man who was not her husband. Third, she was a Samaritan! This was probably the most shocking of all. Jews did not associate with Samaritans. Some would even argue that this encounter with a Samaritan would have rendered Jesus ceremonially unclean.

Nevertheless, in spite of good reasons not to do so, Jesus initiates a conversation with a woman that eventually leads not only to her salvation but to a revival in Samaria! Jesus' behavior doesn't sound like that of someone who would expect his followers to avoid homosexuals.

We must remember the kind of man Jesus was. God wrapped himself in flesh and walked among us. His very incarnation was an act of condescension. None of us was worthy of his coming, nor of his atonement. How dare we look down on another because of the category of his or her sin! Nothing any of us has done is bigger than a dead Jesus! "Christ also died for sins once for all, the just for the unjust, so that He might bring us to God" (1 Peter 3:18).

God used a trip to prison to remind me of this truth the first time I had the privilege of participating in prison ministry. A member of my church invited me in to preach to the inmates at the prison where he was employed. As I drove up to the prison, I was struck by the sterile, ominous feel of the long drive from the main road to the gate. For a while it seemed as though the prison got farther away as I drove. Eventually, I came to the parking lot and walked up to the massive barbed-wire fence. I remember wondering, *Why would a person do anything they knew would land them here? Better yet, why would a person ever do something that would get them sent back?*

As I walked past the third checkpoint, I heard one of the most menacing sounds known to man; the sound of prison bars closing behind me. The place smelled sterile and old at the same time. As the chaplain walked me down to the room where the service was to take place, I watched as inmates walked by. I couldn't help but wonder what each one of them had done to end up in a place like this.

Eventually we came to a gymnasium that had been turned into a sanctuary. Several inmates worked diligently to put the finishing touches on the stage and perform a final sound check on the microphone I would be using. They greeted me with more warmth and enthusiasm than any member of any church I had ever encountered. They were truly grateful that I was there. I was struck as one inmate asked, "Can we get you anything?" I thought to myself, *doesn't he realize that he is in prison?*

As the inmates filed in, there was a tremendous energy and a sense of anticipation unlike any that I had experienced. As the music began, the sound swelled as though the inmates were trying to sing loud enough to knock the walls down. What passion, what enthusiasm . . . what hope! This was a worship experience I would not soon forget.

As I began to preach, the men sat on the edge of their seats as if to hasten the speed at which they would receive each word. They nodded, took notes, shouted "Amen!" It was awesome! At one point, as I addressed the issue of God's holiness and our sinfulness, several of the men began to weep. I remember pausing for a moment, as the Lord seemed to flood my mind with a singular idea. It became painfully obvious to me that there was not an innocent man in the entire room, myself included. I was no better than they were. Christ had shed his blood for me to no less degree than he had for them. We were standing at the foot of the cross and the ground was, indeed, level.

I carry the memory of those men around with me wherever I go. Every now and then, they have to remind me of my standing before God as I deal with my own sense of superiority. They remind me that I, too, am no more than a captive who has been set free, and my freedom is not of my own doing. I am a debtor and a slave to the one who saved me. In the words of that great old hymn:

> This is all my hope and peace,
> Nothing but the blood of Jesus
> This is all my righteousness,
> Nothing but the blood of Jesus.
> O, precious is that flow
> That makes me white as snow!
> No other fount I know,
> Nothing but the blood of Jesus.

Don't forget your job.

There is an old ministry saying that goes, "Remember, we are in sales, not management." The idea is that we should never overstep our bounds. This is also true in witnessing. It is important to remember that the Holy Spirit has already filled the job of convicting people of sin; there are no openings in that department.

There are at least three problems that we incur when we forget this important point. First, we reduce the gospel to a set of legalistic requirements. The person who is told that he or she needs to stop sinning in order to be right with God is often inadvertently taught that salvation is earned. Furthermore, this creates a dependence upon oneself as opposed to reliance upon God to overcome the power of sin.

We see this problem when people say things like, "I am going to get into church as soon as I get some things squared away in my life." Or they might put it another way: "I would come to Christ, but I don't want to be a hypocrite and continue to do the things I do." These are two of the classic statements made by people who do not understand the process through which God handles our sin. The fact is that if we could "get it together" on our own, we wouldn't need God. These statements are similar to my telling people that I am going to try to call my mother in San Antonio from my home in Houston but that before I use a phone, I want to see if I can just yell loud enough. It is humanly impossible for me to yell across two hundred miles. It is equally impossible for me to fix my own sin problem.

The second problem with attempting to convict sinners of their sin is that we interfere with the work of the Spirit. Jesus taught his disciples that when the Spirit came, he would convict the world of sin (John 16:8–11). Thus, any attempt on our part to bring conviction upon a sinner is in essence an overstepping of our bounds. Furthermore, since we are ill-equipped for the job, we are likely to mess it up.

I am not saying that we should ignore sin or avoid speaking on the issue. On the contrary, I cannot adequately communicate the gospel without addressing the issue of sin. The difference comes in that the gospel message is more about *sin* than about sins. The point is that I do not approach a person on the basis of a specific sin that he or she needs to quit but on the basis of a nature that needs to be changed. When I do this, the Holy Spirit will highlight those areas that need to change.

Another difficulty that arises when we play the "stop doing that so you can be saved" game is that we inevitably promote a limited view of sin. There are things in my life that I did not know were sins until I matured enough to discern them from Scripture. Some of them were completely acceptable in the Christian culture in which I was participating at the time. Furthermore, I am sure that some areas in my life still need some ironing out. I have not arrived at sinless perfection. We all have on blinders, and when we push a set of rules, we always miss something obvious.

As a student at Southwestern Seminary, I was exposed to "the mystery of the painting of B. H. Carroll." Carroll was Southwestern's first president. Legend has it that in the original portrait, Carroll was holding a cigar in his hand. This would have been perfectly acceptable in the southeastern part of the United States, where tobacco was king. However, when he became president of a seminary in Texas, the cigar had to go. Thus, if you look closely at the painting, there is what appears to be a cylindrical shadow between Carroll's thumb and first two fingers, where an artist painted over the cigar.

I don't know how much of this legend is factual—maybe none. But the point of it is clear. Some things considered sin in one culture are completely acceptable in another. But God is not a respecter of cultures. God's truth is not dependent upon the changing of time. Nor is God subject to the whims of lawmakers. Thus, it is always best to rely upon the clear teaching of the Bible as opposed to our cultural biases. Our goal is not to be right in the Southeast, or right in the West; our goal is to be right with God.

In short, it is not our job to convict sinners of sin! The goal of a witnessing encounter is to introduce someone to Jesus. The last thing we want is for people to adopt a list of dos and don'ts and confuse them with Christianity. Nor do we wish to present the Christian faith as a set of rules. True Christianity is life-changing. "Therefore if anyone is in Christ, he is a new creature; the old things passed away; behold, new things have come" (2 Corinthians 5:17). This change is not merely external and social; it is essentially internal and supernatural.

I recently preached a series of meetings in a church in the South. We were deep in the heart of the Bible Belt, that part of the country where a person can't get elected dog catcher if he or she does not at least claim affiliation with some church. The services started on Sunday morning and went through Wednesday night. By Monday night, three adult church members had come to faith in Christ!

One woman stood in front of the congregation with tears streaming down her face as she admitted, "I grew up in church, but I never met Jesus." She went on to add, "I learned all the things I was supposed to do and not do, and I just went along." I cannot even list how many times I have heard this same story. I once served on staff with a man who was born again in an evangelistic meeting where he was leading the music! He, too, had grown up in church but had never come to know Christ. When Christianity is presented as a social obligation as opposed to a spiritual transformation, people enter the doors of churches across the country every week thinking they are Christians, when in fact they are not.

Our job is to make sure that people understand who Jesus is and what he came to do. It is the gospel that saves, not our rules and regulations. The Holy Spirit will address our behavior in due time. For some, that will mean an immediate change in their behavior and desires. For others, it will be more gradual as they are exposed to the Word of God and the Spirit exposes their sin.

Don't forget the family name.

I love it when people ask me about my kids. I can't help but brag about how smart and beautiful they are (thanks to my wife). People who haven't seen them always ask, "Are they tall like you and your wife?" or "Which one of you do they most resemble?" It is always assumed that our children will look like us and carry many of our traits. No one ever says, "Do you think they will be like me when they grow up?" That would be ridiculous.

In fact, I often get the funniest looks when I tell people that my mother is only five feet four inches tall. People stare at my large frame and look me in the eyes as if to say, "No, really . . . how tall is she?" The next question usually has something to do with the height of other members in my family. Why? It's simple. People look like—and often act like—their parents! Any other pattern is completely atypical and unexpected. If we are honest, we will admit that meeting a child who doesn't resemble at least one of his parents often raises questions about his parentage.

This is also true of people's expectation of Christ. It is assumed that those who follow Jesus will reflect his character and nature. In fact, all that many people have to go by is us. There are many who have never read a Bible but that hear people call themselves Christian. They know that the name is somehow related to Christ and that it should be indicative of who and what we are. Thus, whatever we do as Christians is often attributed to our Lord. We must keep this danger in mind as we share God's truths with those around us. Our goal is not to foster an arrogance with which we pummel unsuspecting quasi-intellectuals. Our goal is to speak the truth in love.

Not doing so can prove catastrophic. Trust me, I know. As a new Christian I had an encounter with a pair of Jehovah's Witnesses who came calling at my apartment. I was new to the faith and did not have a clue as to what these men represented. I actually thought they were Christians until they turned the conversation to key issues like the deity of Christ and the end times.

I did not have the grasp on the Scriptures that I needed in order to answer them effectively, so I told them to come back. Over the next week I spent more time in the library than I had for any test I had ever taken or any paper I had ever written. When they returned, I was ready. I didn't even wait for their questions. I proceeded to tell them the history of their own organization, the corruption of their founder, the flaws in their theology, and the correct interpretation of the passages they had butchered the week before.

It was a massacre! By the time I finished, they had stopped trying to interrupt and simply stood there in stunned silence. I had just pulled a "spiritual Rambo," and I could not have been more proud. That is, until the two of them left, and I realized that they would never come back. I was rude, arrogant, and a few other things that I can't write in a Christian book. I had won an argument, but lost two souls. I tried to justify what I had done, thinking to myself that at least they heard the truth! However, I knew that my actions and attitude verified every evil expectation they had of Christians.

I don't ever want to be like that again. In fact, I don't want anybody to be like that again. That is one of the main motivations behind this entire chapter. I am not writing this book to produce spiritual Rambos. I would hope that we would be more like one of my daughter's newfound heroes, Mary McLeod Bethune.

One day my daughter Jasmine ran into my study with a book she had been reading for school. She was smiling from ear to ear. She looked like she had just struck gold. She jumped in my lap and erupted, "Daddy, Daddy, let me read you something!" "Sure, Baby," I replied. She opened her book and excitedly began to read the story of Mary McLeod Bethune.

Bethune was the daughter of a sharecropper in the rural South during the early 1900s. Her family, like many sharecroppers, farmed cotton and barely made ends meet. It seemed that no matter how much cotton her father took to market, the money he got was never enough to pay off their debts, let alone provide anything extra.

As a young girl Mary developed an interest in learning. She would steal away to classes taught by a Presbyterian missionary where she learned some basic reading and writing skills. She also learned to work with figures. Soon she could add and subtract. She was very excited, as this was a skill she knew would serve her family well. You see, it was no secret that her father was being cheated at the market. He could neither read nor write. Furthermore, he could not add, subtract, or even read numbers.

One day Mary talked her father into letting her accompany him as he took his cotton to market. As they stood in line, awaiting their turn at the scale, they watched other sharecroppers place their crops on the scale and shake their heads in disappointment as the man reading the scale would inevitably call out a weight far less than expected. Mary was terrified. She did not wish to get her father in trouble, but she also didn't want to see another harvest yield less then they expected. She knew that disagreeing with the men in charge of the weigh-in could literally cost her family their land, if not their lives. She thought fast and came up with a plan.

When Mary's father placed his cotton on the scale, she looked at the scale and yelled excitedly, "Look Daddy, you got four hundred pounds of cotton!" The man at the scale cast a dismayed glance at Mary, then looking at her father, he said, "That's a smart girl you got there." For the first time her father brought home enough money to pay their bills and buy some of the things they desperately needed. As a result, her father allowed her to go away to school. She would eventually become a legend in the field of education, having a college named in her honor.

Mary McLeod Bethune's childhood exploits exemplify what I believe should be the appropriate attitude of the modern American apologist: educated, calculated, and humble. She learned what she needed to know in order to address the needs of her day, namely, how to read the scales at the market. Then, she carefully chose her moment and her strategy. Finally, she did everything she could not to come off as arrogant or confrontational, knowing that the wrong approach would have brought about devastating consequences.

Be educated.

One Christmas, while my mother and I were living with my uncle in South Carolina, he bought me what to this day is still one of my most memorable Christmas gifts. I will never forget diving frantically through the gifts and grabbing that big, brightly wrapped box that had captivated my attention since the moment it was placed beneath the tree. It had my name on it, and I had tried for weeks to figure out what it was. It was too small to be a bike, too large to be a baseball mitt or a football . . . . *What could it be?* I wondered, as I ripped apart the paper. Then, there it was. I could hardly believe my eyes. I looked at my uncle who was almost as excited as I was. "It's a BB gun!" I screamed. "I thought you would like it," he said. "Like it?" I replied, "I love it!" My mother sat in stunned silence, looking at my uncle in disbelief.

As I tore into the box, my uncle dropped the news. "Before you can use that weapon, you must learn to disassemble and reassemble the weapon, clean, carry, and control the weapon, and qualify in the backyard on a target range of my design." Suddenly, my mother and I seemed to exchange expressions. Now she was elated, and I was quite put off. I hoped he would wait a moment and then say, "I'm just kidding, go on and have some fun." However, that statement never came. He meant exactly what he said.

For the next several days, I learned everything there was to know about my pneumatic, single-pump BB pellet rifle. I learned how many moving parts it had. I learned the range at which it could be fired accurately. I learned the damage it could inflict if fired at another person. I learned the damage it could inflict if fired at a window. I learned until I thought there was nothing else to learn, and then I learned some more. At one point I remember thinking, *I don't really want this thing, do I?*

Eventually, it was over. I had met all of my uncle's requirements, and he allowed me to take my rifle outside on my own. It was a glorious day! Words can barely describe how much fun I had shooting cans, bottles, targets and varmints. At first, I had resented my uncle for imposing upon me what I thought were unreasonable requirements. However, I came to realize that what he had done was give me the tools necessary to safely enjoy my gift. No one on the block was as accurate as I was, nor did anyone else have as few mishaps.

The Bible states, "Do your best to present yourself to God as one approved, a workman who does not need to be ashamed and who correctly handles the word of truth" (2 Timothy 2:15 NIV). We would do well to follow Bethune's example by educating ourselves to the fullest extent of our capabilities. Not every Christian must have a theology degree, but every Christian should strive to have a theology.

Unfortunately, statements like this are not readily accepted in many Christian circles. There seems to be a drift toward anti-intellectualism in the modern American church. I remember a conversation that I had several times, with several different people, prior to entering seminary. The theme of all of them was the same. Some well-meaning Christian would look at me and say, "Make sure they don't ruin you up there."

Be calculated.

"Failing to plan is planning to fail." I don't know who said it first, but it is one of those clichés that rings true. It is just as true in contending for Christianity as it is in business. We must have a plan; we must be *calculated*. I will not tell my friend about Jesus if I do not have a plan. I will not give an effective response to the professor who questions my faith if I do not have a plan. I will not respond appropriately to that person on the job whose Jesus stands in stark contrast to the Jesus of the Bible if I do not have a plan. I must have a plan!

Memorize important passages.

The apostle Paul said, "I am not ashamed of the gospel, for it is the power of God for salvation" (Romans 1:16). Again, he says, "All Scripture is God-breathed and is useful for teaching, rebuking, correcting and training in righteousness" (2 Timothy 3:16 NIV). Thus, the most important tool in sharing our faith in Christ with others is the Bible.

There are many presentation styles available that will prepare you to share your faith. Personally, I don't think it makes much difference which one you use, or whether you choose not to use any at all—as long as you commit to memory the key passages concerning the person and work of Jesus Christ.

Seize divine appointments.

George Whitefield once said, "God forbid that I should travel with anybody a quarter of an hour without speaking of Christ to them." Bill Bright believed that anytime he had five minutes alone with someone, God had just given him a chance to share his faith. It is this attitude that made both men great evangelists.

You don't have to be a Whitefield or a Bright to be serious about taking advantage of the opportunities God provides. All you need is a commitment beforehand. If you make a commitment prior to the opportunity, you will be much more likely to seize the moment when it comes.

Anticipate objections.

Not everyone will agree with what you say. The best way to handle objections is to anticipate them. Ask yourself, "What is a question that someone is likely to ask when I make this assertion?" Then wrestle with the question until you come up with a reasonable response. This way you will be less likely to be caught off guard when the question is raised—and, trust me, it will be.

Ask questions and listen to the answers.

Everybody believes something, and if you give them a chance, they will probably tell you exactly what it is. I love it when people tilt their heads and get that philosophical look on their faces; you know, the one that implies. "I am about to say something so profound that it will prove my superior intelligence and change your life." If we are not careful, our tendency is to immediately dismiss what they say. That is the wrong move! Listen to them. In fact, listen intently. Soak up every word.

Find out exactly what it is they believe about life, death, sin, judgment, and Jesus. Then, once they have explained their positions, ask probative questions. "I see. So you believe Jesus is just another teacher? How do you reconcile that with his personal claims to divinity?" Or, "OK, you think everyone should just do whatever works for them at the time. Does that also mean you want to do away with the criminal justice system?"

If the Bible is true (and it is), then Christianity is the only viable worldview. Hence, every other worldview will eventually break down at some fundamental point. There will either be internal logical inconsistency, or there will be a problem with the viability of the worldview as it relates to the real world. For example, the Buddhist who argues that sin is not real will eventually have to do one of two things: Either he will have to call evil good, or he will have to find another worldview because his is no longer viable in the real world.

Take your time.

All my life I have dreamed of being a lawyer. In fact, before I started preaching, I was an international business major. My goal was to finish college, go to law school, and practice some form of international law. I could just see myself arguing cases before the Supreme Court, and winning every time. But God had other plans.

So there I was, a young lawyer-to-be let loose on an unsuspecting world of non-Christians whom I was sure I would win to Jesus one by one if necessary. I actually had a great deal of success early on. I would share with people, and most of them would be ready to receive Jesus. However, it did not take long for me to run into an unwilling soul.

I couldn't believe it! I had shared the biblical truths, some archeological truths, and some logical truths. I had answered his objections and exposed the weaknesses in his worldview. I had even shared my personal story, but nothing seemed to get through. "Where did I go wrong?" I asked one of my mentors. He sat me down and asked, "How long did it take you to get it?" I was floored. How soon I had forgotten! It had taken me weeks to evaluate the things I had heard and come to faith in Christ. Furthermore, as discussed earlier, there is the matter of the Holy Spirit and his role in the regeneration process.

I needed to learn to take my time. Some people have been "prepped," as it were, for our encounters. Others are prepped *by* our encounters. Unfortunately, though, there are many more people for whom our encounter will be just one more nail in their proverbial coffin. They are part of the many who enter the broad gate, as opposed to the narrow one. I cannot know which is the case, so my role is simply to take my time and take full advantage of every opportunity I am given to speak the truth in love.

Be wise.

As the task of completing this manuscript draws near, I am watching the opening days of the war with Iraq. There are several things that strike me. First, I cannot believe the level of media coverage. Every minute of every day there is a live feed from some location inside Iraq; there are members of the media embedded in forward units; there are cameras in planes, tanks, buildings, and bombs.

Second, I am impressed with the manner in which the government continues to inform the public. Every day combat generals, members of the Joint Chiefs of Staff, the secretary of state, the secretary of defense, and the White House spokesman stand in front of the cameras, give updates, and take questions. What I find amazing is the care with which every word is chosen. A reporter will say, "Yesterday, you said. . . ." The government official then retorts, "No, what I said was. . . ." It's amazing. It is also evidence of the fact that what these men and women say is not "off the cuff," even though their statements are not prepared. They stand and speak in their own words. They deftly handle hostile questions; they nimbly avoid traps set by reporters, such as those questions whose answers would compromise tactical secrets; they respond in a manner that impugns the reporter's question rather than the official's avoidance of the question.

What we see is the result of preparation and wisdom. These men and women know what they are going to say and how they are going to say it. They also anticipate questions that will arise and prepare appropriate answers to those questions beforehand. Hence, they rarely appear to be caught off guard. I am not suggesting that we should be as curt as Secretary Rumsfeld, or as matter-of-fact as General Tommy Franks. I am merely suggesting that we think through what we are going to say and anticipate objections in order to "be ready to give an answer to anyone who asks."

Conclusion
WHAT, THEN, SHALL WE DO?

C ultural apologists usually advocate one of three approaches to the issues that are currently redefining the culture in which we live. Either we can be isolated from our culture, immersed in our culture, or insulated in the midst of our culture. Each of these approaches can be illustrated by a diver's relationship to the water. The diver who jumps in without gear represents immersion. The diver with a wet suit and scuba gear represents insulation—in the water but protected from and unaffected by it. A man on the shore who refuses to dive into the water represents isolation.

Cultural immersion is the easiest approach to the culture because it is the most natural. We were born into this culture. It was here that we learned how to think, act, and react. It was here that we developed our worldview. It was here that we were educated. In fact, it is not until we come to faith in Christ that we even know that there is an alternative. Many Christians grew up in a church environment that was completely immersed in the culture and could not tell the difference between the two worldviews if their life depended on it.

Cultural *immersion* is the de facto approach for most Christians. In doing nothing (and in being ignorant of the philosophical shift around them), most Christians have simply adopted the philosophical assumptions promulgated by the adversary. They have become "all things to all people." They parrot popular phrases without weighing their implications—the church member who never shares her faith with the Muslim coworker because "we all worship the same God"; the college student who sees nothing wrong with his philosophy professor's assertion that "there are no absolutes"; the Episcopal bishops who elect an openly gay Bishop of New Hampshire. These people unwittingly accept the immersion approach because the Bible has been usurped by our culture.

The greatest benefit this approach offers is acceptance within the culture. When Christians share the same philosophical assumptions, values, roles, norms and mores of the culture, they meet little resistance in our culture. These Christians are not called intolerant, narrow-minded bigots. They do not turn off lost people.

The "seeker-driven" emphasis within the modern Church Growth movement is another example. These churches' main goal is to create an environment with the "seeker" in mind. Their pulpit is removed because it represents authority. No one on staff wears a shirt and tie because doing so would represent the uptight, "old fashioned" way of doing church. The preacher becomes the "speaker" or "communicator." The sermon becomes a "talk." Biblical exposition gives way to the seventeen-minute topical, self-help sounding, felt-needs based pop psychology with full multimedia support. Songs of Zion are replaced with top-forty cover songs. The call to repentance and faith is supplanted by an invitation to "make yourself at home." Ultimately, biblical community is abandoned in favor of a country club—all in the name of reaching a group of people the Bible says do not even exist (see Romans 3:11).

The obvious drawback to cultural immersion is that it offers no alternative. This position allows the sinner to feel comfortable in his or her sin. It compromises the gospel message. This approach loses the game before it even starts because it has bought in to philosophical assumptions with which the gospel message is completely incongruent.

Isolation, on the other hand, represents complete withdrawal from the culture. "Come out from their midsts and be separate" is the battle cry of the isolationist (2 Corinthians 6:17). This position is based on the idea that interaction with the culture will corrupt those who walk with Christ. Isolationism has several strengths.

First, isolation offers a clear distinction between Christianity and the culture, and thus a clear alternative. It may be difficult to choose between a Chevy pickup and a GMC, but put a Ford or a Dodge in the mix and things change. Suddenly the differences are more clear and the choice more obvious. Isolation creates distance between "us" and "them."

Second, isolation protects Christians from corruption, or at least appears to do so. If we don't interact with the culture, the culture cannot corrupt us; or so the argument goes. This preserves the integrity of the message. The culture's philosophy cannot influence our thinking if we avoid the culture altogether.

Of course, the flip side of this is the fact that isolation not only eliminates the culture's influence on the church, it also negates godly cultural transformation. This requires interaction. Unfortunately, to some isolationists, any interaction represents compromise.

The extreme corporate expression of isolation is the traditional church. Every church has tradition, but the traditional church is so steeped in its tradition that it would rather die than adapt. An observant person can script these services after a couple of weeks. You know: three hymns and a special followed by three points, a poem, an altar call, and a handshake at the back door. This church was once a pillar of the community, but it is rapidly becoming an albatross. This church is proud that time has passed it by, but it still can't understand why young families aren't coming. This is the church that will only hire a young pastor if he acts like an old man and will throw him off the nearest cliff if he ever forgets his place and tries to change something.

Insulation is the process of being "in the world, but not of the world." This is often viewed as the middle ground. Here we interact with the culture, but we do so with the protection of our wet suit, or our submarine. In other words, we get close to the world, but we never actually make contact.

I am not, however, asking you to choose between insulation, isolation, or immersion. I don't find any of these solutions totally sufficient. I believe that we should *infiltrate and invade* the culture. To infiltrate means to enter enemy territory without being detected. To invade means to enter by force in order to conquer. I believe the task at hand requires both. Furthermore, I believe that if we are to infiltrate and invade our culture with the truth, we will have to employ each of the three previous techniques. We must get our hands dirty in people's lives like those committed to immersion; keep the lines clearly drawn like the isolationist; all the while exemplifying the balance of the insulation approach.

In my mind I see a picture of an allied camp set up in the midst of enemy territory. As such we are completely distinct from our surroundings but able to blend in as necessary. Occasionally we venture out into enemy territory for reconnaissance purposes, but we never become completely comfortable, and we always come back home.

Politics

Many contemporary discussions of Christian involvement in politics take a similar turn toward "electing the right people." As the argument goes, "If we just get the right man in the White House (or Governor's Mansion, Supreme Court, etc.), the tide will turn." While I agree that we should participate in elections with a view toward casting a vote for the person whose platform lines up closest with a biblical worldview, I do not believe that this is the chief end of Christian involvement in the political process. In fact, this view has often led to great compromise. At times believers will gloss over very important aspects of a candidate's character in order to elect "the lesser of two evils." In such instances our prophetic voice is at least muffled, if not silenced altogether.

How many times do we have to hear "Christian politicians" extol the virtues of "choosing his or her words carefully in order to avoid offending the electorate" before we realize that the compromise usually follows them into the office to which they are seeking to be elected. How long must we celebrate partial victories and conciliation at the expense of speaking the truth in love? I want the right people in office as much as the next guy, but I also realize that the battle does not belong to elected officials; the battle is yours; it is mine; and ultimately, it's the Lord's.

In the area of abortion, for example, I would love to see the laws in this land reflect God's truth. However, I realize that such a change would only serve to restrain individuals from carrying out such depraved acts; it would not remove the depravity. Only the gospel, as it is faithfully and effectively communicated by blood-washed, Spirit-filled, biblically equipped believers can both change depraved actions and cleanse a depraved soul. I am afraid that victories on the legal front would only lead to further justification of our silence in the public square. Why would we need to speak up for righteousness in the schoolyard, in the break room, or at the coffee table if we believe it has been achieved through legislation?

Christian involvement in politics currently reflects an infiltrate-and-assimilate mentality as opposed to infiltrate-and-invade. We have become so intent on doing and saying the things necessary to win elections that we have forgotten the next step: serving the Lord with the position. Moreover, those of us outside of public office have become so dependent upon elected officials that we have forgotten our place. We must actively engage our culture in the marketplace of ideas. We must stay on top of current affairs. We must develop a Christian worldview through which we evaluate current events, and we must communicate our position in an effective manner. I may not be able to win an election, but I can win the mind of a neighbor or two.

Science

My dear friend Art is a surgeon. He is one of my heroes. He is a member of a rare minority, not because he is a black surgeon but because he is a committed Christian who has distinguished himself in a scientific field. Art has a master's degree in microbiology as well as a doctor of medicine degree. He is currently mastering the field of general surgery where he routinely does, among other things, bypass surgery. He is one of those rare blends of an unwavering commitment to Christ coupled with the intelligence and intensity necessary to excel in a scientific field. Moreover, Art has the respect of his peers and his patients. His peers recognize his competence and keen intellect, while his patients know that he is a physician who spends as much time on his face before God on their behalf as he does with his face in the latest medical journals. Unfortunately, Art is a rare breed.

There is perhaps no area in greater need of infiltration and invasion by Christian ambassadors than the sciences. In fact, this area has fallen so far off of the church's radar that it is unusual to meet young Christians who aspire to study or work in scientific fields. Moreover, many Christians actually believe that there is a great line of demarcation between faith and science—hence the continued dearth of Christian scientists. As a result, many young Christians spend their high school days confused as their science teachers extol the virtues of naturalistic materialism and its cohort, Darwinian evolution. These same young people spent their early years at the university reeling as their biology professors attempt to complete the coup.

It is as though we have been beaten into submission. We have given up. Science is not for us; let's look elsewhere. Wait a minute! God created this universe. Who is better equipped than those of us who know him to explore and discover its vast complexities? Christians belong in the sciences. In fact, not being there is poor stewardship on our part. We must raise up a generation of Christian ambassadors who know that there is a seat for them at the table of scientific discovery and who are willing to do what it takes to get there.

Higher Education

In addition to the sciences, Christians are shockingly absent in higher education. On the university level, there seems to be an inverse relationship between a school's pursuit of God and its pursuit of academic excellence. How else can we explain the fact that none of our nation's top schools have maintained its theological moorings, and several of our most respected Christian institutions appear to be mired in theological liberalism?

This is not easy for me to say. I love the body of Christ, and I am committed to higher education. Nevertheless, the truth must be acknowledged. Most Christian schools are not necessarily "good schools." Our thirteen-year-old daughter is beginning to talk about college, and the sad reality is that there is an obvious yet unwritten rule: The higher the level of academic excellence a university has achieved, the lower its level of Christian conviction. At times it seems as though we must make a trade. We can either aim for the academic stratosphere (and give up on the idea of Christ-centered university education), or we can give up on the idea of academic excellence in favor of a thoroughly faith-based, Christ-centered experience.

Some would argue that the academic ranking of schools is too subjective to make such an argument. However, I am not talking about subjective criteria like a school's "academic reputation." I am talking about measurable, objective criteria like library size, computer access, student-to-faculty ratio, research facilities, research grants, professors with terminal degrees, professors with academic publications and membership in academic societies. Christian institutions are woefully short in these areas. Of course, there are exceptions. For example, Union University in Tennessee and Biola in California are among the handful of schools that have compromised neither academics nor strong evangelical convictions, but the list is far too short. These are exceptions, not the rule.

My goal here is not to condemn Christian colleges and universities. I am simply pointing out the urgent need for infiltration and invasion of the culture in higher education. Imagine the potential impact of Christian universities with indefatigable commitment to biblical Christianity and a pursuit of academic excellence that rivals that of Harvard, Stanford, and Princeton. What an amazing training ground for the Christian ambassadors of tomorrow! What an amazing testimony to the culture at large that is convinced that following Christ is an act of intellectual suicide.

The Next Generation

I love to people-watch. I could sit for hours and simply observe people passing by. I love to watch people's mannerisms and expressions and try to figure out what they are thinking. I enjoy listening to accents and trying to figure out where they're from. One of my favorite places to people-watch is the airport. I have gotten to the point where I can tell the difference between the casual business traveler and the hard-core road warrior. I can pick out the first-time flyer with a single glance. I can also tell the difference between a couple who just got away for some much-needed R&R and a couple who just had a vacation that turned into a war zone.

Recently, though, I had the rare privilege for which all people-watchers secretly long. I actually saw something that I had never seen before! I was about to board one of those regional jets that men my size absolutely loathe. As a frequent flyer I am usually extended the courtesy of boarding first. This time, however, since I was seated in the first seat and didn't wish to be beaten about the head and shoulders by every person who followed me onto the airplane, I waited until everyone else was on before I boarded.

As I sat watching the passengers board the plane (a particular treat for a people-watcher), a woman and her son caught my eye. He was about sixteen years old and was flying alone. His mother was fussing over him as mothers do when they are about to put their sons on an airplane. It was the usual stuff; she wiped off his face, ran her hands through his hair and kissed him (all of which 16-year-old boys abhor), then she grabbed his right hand and moved it from his forehead to his chest, then from one shoulder to the other and up to his mouth. Suddenly, I realized what she was doing. She was making the sign of the cross.

As I watched the scene unfold, the boy's body language told a story that I could not wait to retell. While he was respectful and obedient in allowing his mother to forcibly make the sign of the cross using *his* hand, it was obvious that he did not like it. His arm was a bit stiff, his posture submissive yet agitated. He glanced off as if to see who was watching, and he pulled his hand away as soon as she was done. Afterward he hugged her neck and kissed her goodbye. This was about more than a boy being forced to perform a ritual; it was bigger than a mother's anxiety over air travel or distance between her and her son. This encounter was a microcosm of one of our greatest obstacles to transferring faith from generation to generation. This encounter taught me at least three lessons as it relates to my desire as a father to see my faith impact my children and my children's children.

First, this encounter shows us the futility of transferring ritualistic faith. This young man was being forced to perform a ritual that obviously did not mean as much to him as it did to his mother. I know we nonliturgical Christians will be tempted to attribute this to a ritualistic religion based on mystical symbols and practices, but slow down a minute. I doubt this boy was resisting on theological grounds.

More than likely, he was objecting to something that he simply did not understand and thus did not value. In that regard, there is no difference between him and the son of a Baptist or Methodist who does not understand the value of baptism, church attendance, financial stewardship, or anything else that we sometimes ritualize. If all we communicate is the *what* without the *why*, we run the risk of offering our children what to them is no more than dead ritual.

Second, this encounter shows us the perils of borrowed faith. What was more frightening to me than the young man's rejection of a ritual was the likelihood of his rejection of God. If our children view our faith as dead ritual, they will probably dismiss our God as myth, fairytale, or legend. If our faith is tied up in the things we do and not the passionate pursuit of a personal God, why should the next generation want it? Moreover, why should we?

Finally, this encounter foreshadows the failure of the transference of faith from one generation to the next. As I watched this young man get on the plane, I could not help but follow this encounter through to its logical (although not guaranteed) conclusion. I saw him in a college classroom sitting in front of a distinguished-looking biology professor to whom he must refer using the esteemed honorific "Dr." and from whom he expects to receive the knowledge necessary to understand and operate in the world. I saw that professor extolling the virtues of naturalism and materialism as he systematically picked this boy's borrowed faith apart piece by piece.

I saw that same young man going from that biology class to a philosophy course, where another professor with more degrees than this young man could want and more knowledge than he thought one person could have, ran through the history of philosophical thought, carefully analyzing among other things the "illogic and naiveté" of religious faith.

From there I imagined him heading off to a psychology course where he learned that man's greatest problem is not sin but self-image; that sexual roles, norms and mores are up for grabs; that guilt is inappropriate; and that a negative childhood not only dooms us to a life of mediocrity and/or deviance but also excuses it.

To top it all off, I envisioned this same young man heading to a religion course, where a professor who by his very position is presumed to have examined every corner of the Christian faith with the objectivity of a judge and the precision of a surgeon proceeds to demythologize creation, call Adam and Eve into question, deny the flood, berate the patriarchs, assign Paul to the ranks of the politically incorrect, spiritualize the resurrection, and strip Jesus of every vestige of divinity.

As this young man faces this borage, the only thing he has to cling to is his mother's well-meaning ritual. What does he internalize? Will it be the men and women of titles and distinction, or the mother who forced him to make the sign of the cross so she wouldn't feel so scared when he boarded an airplane?

Our culture is hostile to Christian faith. We no longer live in a time or a place where what we believe constitutes the norm, or even an accepted point of view. What we believe flies in the

face of the cherished principles of religious relativism, tolerance, and philosophical pluralism. We are considered
"untrained and uneducated" men and women from whom our
culture needs to be protected. We are the modern version of
Peter and John standing before a Sanhedrin armed with television and radio stations, colleges and universities, newspapers
and books, all being leveraged against "the faith that was once
for all handed down to the saints." Struggle is inevitable.
Conflict is at hand. Will we bow before the god of culture? Or
will we plant our feet, square our shoulders, lift our heads, and
give an account to all those who ask us not just what we believe
but why?

NOTES

Chapter 1

1. Sally Morgenthaler, *Worship Evangelism* (Grand Rapids: Zondervan Publishing House, 1995), 20.

2. This estimate was made by George Barna in Morganthaler, *Worship Evangelism*, 20.

3. Robert Gundry, *A Survey of the New Testament* (Grand Rapids: Zondervan Publishing House, 1970), 51.

4. Craig S. Keener, *The IVP Bible Background Commentary: New Testament* (Downers Grove, IL: InterVarsity Press, 1993), 333.

5. John Calvin, *Acts*, The Crossway Classic Commentaries, Alistar McGrath and J. I. Packer, eds. (Wheaton: Crossway Books, 1995), 64.

6. Luke Timothy Johnson, *The Real Jesus: The Misguided Quest for the Historical Jesus and the Truth of the Traditional Gospels* (San Francisco: Harper SanFrancisco, 1996), 64. Johnson's book is a direct response to the controversial research of the Jesus Seminar.

7. John Shelby Spong, *A New Christianity for a New World: Why Traditional Faith is Dying and How a New Faith Is Being Born* (San Francisco: Harper SanFrancisco, 2001), 4–5.

8. Ibid.

9. Ibid., 6–7.

10. Marcus J. Borg, *Meeting Jesus Again for the First Time: The Historical Jesus and the Heart of Contemporary Faith* (San Francisco: Harper SanFrancisco, 1994), 6.

11. Ibid., 8.

12. http://www.usconstitution.net/jeffwall.html (accessed August 12, 2003).

13. David Barton, "The Separation of Church and State," Web-based article accessed at http://www.wallbuilders.com/ resources/search/detail.php:ResourceID=9 (accessed March 6, 2003).

14. Ibid.

15. Anti-Defamation League statement on the Internet, accessed at www.Adl.org/10comm/conclusion.asp (accessed December 15, 2002).

Chapter 2

1. Philip Johnson, *Reason in the Balance: The Case Against Naturalism in Science, Law and Education* (Downers Grove, IL: InterVarsity Press, 1995), 37. Johnson is a graduate of Harvard Law School, former Supreme Court clerk, and law professor of the University of California at Berkley. His work is on the cutting edge of the debate about truth. His books include *The Wedge of Truth: Defeating Darwinism by Opening Minds.*

2. Ibid.

3. Ibid., 38.

4. For a pertinent discussion, see Josh McDowell and Bob Hostetler, *The New Tolerance: How a Cultural Movement Threatens to Destroy You, Your Faith, and Your Children* (Wheaton, IL: Tyndale House, 1998).

5. David Bosch, *Transforming Mission: Paradigm Shifts in Theology of Mission,* American Society of Missiology Series, number 16 (Maryknoll, NY: Orbis Books, 1992), 321. Bosch offers a thorough discussion of modernism, alluding to the work of Descartes, Bacon, Newton and others, but for the

purposes of this paper, his premise about the roots of the move-ment will suffice.

6. Ibid., 350.

7. David Harvey, *The Condition of Postmodernity* (Oxford: Blackwell, 1990), 11–12. Harvey is writing from a secular and Marxist perspective. Thus, both the motivation and philosophy behind his assessments differ greatly from other works con-sulted herein. Nevertheless, his assessment of postmodernism is both poignant and timely.

8. Ibid.

9. Ibid.

10. See Lesslie Newbegin, *The Gospel in a Pluralist Society* (London: Holy Trinity Church, 1989), 2.

11. Ibid., 5.

12. Harvey, *The Condition of Postmodernity*, 41.

13. By "philosophical response," we do not mean to single out philosophy, although philosophy was a key area affected by the change. We use this term to demonstrate the nature of the movement as a shift in the way that one thinks about the ulti-mate nature of things.

14. Bosch, *Transforming Mission*, 531. Bosch points to his dependence on Küng at this point.

15. Ibid.

16. See D. A. Carson, *The Gagging of God: Christianity Confronts Pluralism* (Grand Rapids: Zondervan, 1996), 13–22. These three distinctions are alluded to in other works, but Carson gives them the most attention, and actually categorizes them. Thus, we borrow these distinctions from him.

17. Roger Greenway and Timothy M. Monsma, *Cities: Mission's New Frontier* (Grand Rapids: Baker Book House, 1989), 13. Cities are growing at a rate three times that of their rural counterparts. Thus, although rural areas are obviously becom-ing more pluralistic, empirical pluralism is largely an urban

phenomenon. This trend will have tremendous implications on the future of missiology.

18. Carson, *The Gagging of God*, 14. It is also the second largest black nation, and soon to become the third largest Hispanic nation. This trend is also being experienced in other parts of the Western world, such as Britain and Canada.

19. Ibid., 18–19. Carson does not offer much discussion at this point. He merely uses this term as a step between empirical and philosophical pluralism. For further development, we infer from his later discussions.

20. Ibid., 18.

21. Ibid.

22. Ibid., 19. Emphasis is his.

23. Ibid. The logic of such an argument will be addressed later in this discussion. Nevertheless, it is important to state that it represents a philosophically untenable position. However, deconstructionism and the new hermeneutic make it plausible (to some) to make such assertions regardless of their philosophical implications on one's overall worldview. For a further critique, see Norman L. Geisler, "Jacques Derrida," *Baker Encyclopedia of Christian Apologetics* (Grand Rapids: Baker Books, 1999), 192–94.

24. Newbigin, *The Gospel in a Pluralist Society*, 14.

25. Geisler, "Jacques Derrida," 192–94. Geisler states that although Derrida was merely synthesizing the work of Kant (metaphysics), Nietzsche (atheism), Wittgenstein (view of language), Husserl (phenomenological method), Heidegger (existentialism), and James (pragmatism), he was the first to offer a cogent argument for deconstruction.

26. C. S. Lewis, *The Case for Christianity* (New York: Simon & Schuster, 1996), 3. This volume was originally published in Great Britain with the title *Broadcast Talks*.

27. Ibid., 4.

28. Ibid., 4–5.

Chapter 3

1. Johnson, *The Real Jesus,* 77. Concerning *religio licita,* see Robert Gundry, *A Survey of the New Testament* (Grand Rapids: Zondervan Publishing House, 1970), 224–25.

2. Johnson, *The Real Jesus,* 77.

3. *Bias: A CBS Insider Exposes How the Media Distorts the News* (Washington, DC: Regnery Publishing, 2002).

Chapter 4

1. "ADA Quick Guide to Religious Displays," http://www.adl.org/issue_education/decemberdilemma.pdf (accessed September 15, 2003).

2. "Rutherford Institute Defends Honor Guardsman Fired for Offering God's Blessing at Graveside Military Funerals," March 6, 2003, http://www.rutherford.org/articles_db/press_release.asp?article_id=343 (accessed September 15, 2003).

Chapter 7

1. Dietrich Bonhoeffer, *The Cost of Discipleship,* trans. R. H. Fuller (New York: Macmillan, 1958), 7.

2. Jonathan Edwards, *Religious Affections: A Christian's Character before God,* James M. Houston, ed. (Portland, OR: Multnomah, 1984), 3.

3. Ibid, 4.

4. Ibid.

5. Ibid.

6. A. W. Tozer, *The Root of the Righteous,* 137.

Chapter 8

1. Bruce M. Metzger, *The Text of the New Testament: Its Transmission, Corruption and Restoration* (Oxford: Oxford University Press, 1992), 38, 39. The document as Metzger reproduces it on page 52 contains a few verses from the Fourth Gospel.

2. Ibid., 67. Metzger is referring to the "Old Syriac" version. See also Paul Little, *Know Why You Believe* (Downers Grove, IL: InterVarsity Press, 1968).

3. Ibid., 87.

Chapter 9

1. See http://www.beliefnet.com/features/searchforjesus/ resurrection/ resurrection1.asp/.